Articles by **David Fantle**

This publication is not for sale in the E.C. and/or Australia or New Zealand.

ISBN 0-7935-4762-8

7777 W. Bluemound Rd. P.O. Box 13819 Milwaukee, WI 53213

CONTENTS

THE SHOWS

THE ADDAMS FAMILY

ABC, 1964-66 (64 episodes)

Theme Song: "The Addams Family Theme" by Vic Mizzy

Major cast members: Carolyn Jones, John Astin, Jackie Coogan, Ted Cassidy, Lisa Loring, Ken Weatherwax, Blossom Rock, Felix Silla, Rolf Sedan, Margaret Hamilton, Thing

Now let's get this straight: Thing, the human right hand was the family servant on "The Addams Family," and Spot, the fire-breathing dragon was the family pet that lived under the stairwell on "The Munsters." Considering both shows premiered the same year and were canceled less than a week apart, it's easy to get the two confused. "The Addams Family," based on the macabre drawings of Charles Addams in *The New Yorker,* featured the comedic eccentricities of Gomez (John Astin) and Morticia (Carolyn Jones) Addams and their ghoulish offspring, Pugsley (Ken Weatherwax) and Wednesday (Lisa Loring). The supporting cast of misfits included Uncle Fester (Jackie Coogan), their zombie-like butler Lurch (Ted Cassidy), and the human hair ball, Cousin Itt (Felix Silla). A typical episode would find Gomez blowing up his model trains or Uncle Fester fishing with dynamite, illuminating a light bulb in his mouth or riding around the house in a motorcycle. As the finger-snapping theme song goes, "they're creepy and they're kooky, mysterious and spooky . . ." The show spun off years later into an animated Saturday morning series. More recently the Addams were given new life with two financially successful motion pictures featuring an entirely new cast.

Gomez, Morticia and the clan.

George Reeves and Phyllis Coates.

THE ADVENTURES OF SUPERMAN

Syndicated, 1953-57 (104 episodes)

Theme Song: "Superman" by Leon Klatzkin

Major cast members: George Reeves, Phyllis Coates (1951), Noel Neill (1953-57), Jack Larson, John Hamilton, Robert Shayne

"Up in the sky. It's a bird. It's a plane. No, it's Superman!" And with those famous opening lines Superman was "up, up and away to fight for truth justice and the American way." There are probably more popular catch phrases associated with this show than any other series. Part of that is due to the fact that Superman had a long life before this program. It was born as a comic book, but also appeared in the newspaper comics and on radio (with Bud Collyer as the "Man of Steel."). On television, the mild-mannered reporter for *The Daily Planet* who did the quick change into Superman tights was George Reeves. Clark had one of those taboo office romances (or did he?) with fellow reporter, Lois Lane (Phyllis Coates for year one, Noel Neill afterward). Besides Lois, his only other weakness was the foreign mineral known as kryptonite, from the planet Krypton. Otherwise, Superman kept the peace in Metropolis. The special effects seem cheesy by today's standards (look closely, and you can see the rope enabling Superman to fly). Years after the show ended, Superman (this time Christopher Reeve) came back in a series of big budget movies. In the '90s, a new TV series, "The Adventures of Lois and Clark" put more emphasis on the romantic relationship between the two reporters.

ALFRED HITCHCOCK PRESENTS

CBS, NBC, 1955-1965 (361 episodes)

Theme Song: "Funeral March of a Marionette" by Charles Gounod

Host: Alfred Hitchcock; Big name guests: Steve McQueen, Joanne Woodward, Dick York, Peter Lorre, Dick Van Dyke, Robert Redford, Claude Rains

In one of the most memorable opening sequences in TV history, Alfred Hitchcock entered the TV screen to fill a silhouette line drawing of his profile. The theme music, an adaptation of a classical piece by Gounod, played in the background. Then, in his very stuffy and sardonic British manner, he bid his audience "Good ev'ning." As if to show a disdain for TV's commercialization, he used the advertising breaks to take digs at his sponsors, describing them as "a one-minute anesthetic," "calculated but confusing" and "tedious." Initially, the advertisers didn't find these characterizations too funny. The "Master of the Macabre" played host each week to a different melodrama, starring both established names (Peter Lorre, Claude Rains) and young up-and-comers (Steve McQueen, Robert Redford). His staff poured over some 400 novels each season to come up with the 32 teleplays. Although master filmmaker Hitchcock only directed 20 of the some 361 episodes, each suspense anthology was consistently well-acted, well-written and well-directed. As executive producer, he did maintain creative control over the final product. In 1962, the program was expanded to one hour and in 1985, five years after Hitchcock's death, colorized versions of his openings were used to introduce new episodes. How deliciously macabre!

The great man usually introduced the show with a prop against a plain background.

The ageless Mr. Clark.

AMERICAN BANDSTAND

ABC, 1957-1987

Theme Song: "Bandstand Boogie" by Charles Albertine

Host: Dick Clark

In 1956, a Philadelphia disc jockey named Dick Clark hosted a local TV rock 'n' roll show called "Bandstand." Soon the program graduated to network status, became known as "American Bandstand" and went on to become a television institution. For the first six years the series aired daily for the kids returning home from school. For the final 24 years, the program ran on Saturday mornings. Some of the performers who received their first national exposure on "American Bandstand" include Bobby Darin, the Jackson Five, the Mamas and the Papas, the Osmond Brothers, Dionne Warwick and many others. During its 30 year run, the show's format remained constant: a performer would lip-synch a record, a panel of teenage judges would give a numerical ranking (between 35 and 98) to the new singles ("I like the beat"), and the studio audience danced . . . and danced. The format was not the only thing to remain constant for 30 years. The show's host, the seemingly ageless Clark, remained remarkably hip and youthful-looking considering many of the acts were young enough to be his children. "Bandstand Boogie," was originally a hit for Les Elgert in 1954. Two years later it was used by Clark as the show's theme. Lyrics were added years later by Barry Manilow and Bruce Sussman.

The compassionate surgeon, Vince Edwards.

BEN CASEY

ABC, 1961-66 (153 episodes)

Theme Song: "Theme from Ben Casey" by David Raksin

Major cast members: Vince Edwards, Sam Jaffe, Bettye Ackerman, Harry Landers, Nick Dennis, Jeanne Bates, Stella Stevens (1965), Ben Piazza (1965), Franchot Tone (1965-66), Jim McMullan (1965-66), Marilyn Mason (1965-66)

Long before the stark realism of "ER" there was "Ben Casey." Still considered one of the finest medical dramas in TV history, it starred Vince Edwards as the young and virile surgeon, Dr. Ben Casey. Edwards was discovered by, of all people—Bing Crosby, whose production company produced the series. Although the young Dr. Casey was almost as brainy as "Doogie Howser," he still occasionally sought the wisdom and guidance of County General Hospital's chief surgeon, Dr. David Zorba (Sam Jaffe). Known for its innovative use of the camera, including tight close-ups during tense moments, the show also tackled some fairly controversial topics for its day. Some changes came to the hospital in the show's last season, including a new chief surgeon, Dr. Daniel Niles Freeland (played by veteran film actor Franchot Tone). Casey was even allowed a love affair. But this was no conventional romance. The object of his affections was a beautiful young woman (Stella Stevens) who had just awakened from a 13-year coma. They must have had a lot of catching up to do! That's why it took five episodes to develop this blossoming romance. "Ben Casey" checked out of County General in 1966 after a long and highly rated run on ABC.

THE BEVERLY HILLBILLIES

CBS, 1962-1971 (216 episodes)

Theme Song: "Ballad of Jed Clampett" by Paul Henning

Major cast members: Buddy Ebsen, Irene Ryan, Donna Douglas, Max Baer Jr., Raymond Bailey, Harriet MacGibbon (1962-69), Nancy Kulp

CBS founder William Paley built a reputation for his good taste and high programming standards. He built the finest news organization in television with such stellar journalists as Edward R. Murrow, Eric Severeid and Walter Cronkite. He also introduced the masses to regular doses of classical music, featuring the world's finest musicians. So how did "The Beverly Hillbillies" ever slip into his network lineup? Paley also believed in giving the audience what they wanted. And in the case of "The Beverly Hillbillies," the proof is in the ratings. For its first two seasons, this goofy sitcom was the number one show in the country, attracting as many as 60 million viewers a week. The storyline was simple: After oil was mistakingly discovered by Jed Clampett (Buddy Ebsen) on his Appalachian spread, his kinfolk said, "Jed move away from here." So he loaded up the family and "moved to Beverly—Hills that is." The Clampett clan included widower Jed's mother-in-law Granny (Irene Ryan), his daughter Elly May (Donna Douglas), and his nephew, Jethro Bodine (Max Baer Jr., the prize fighter's son). The plots usually concerned the cultural clashes between the Clampetts and the good folks of Beverly Hills, particularly, their banker, the befuddled Mr. Drysdale (Raymond Bailey) and his secretary, the proper and stuffy Miss Hathaway (Nancy Kulp). In the '90s, "The Beverly Hillbillies" was made into a not-so-successful feature film. The program's opening song, written by the show's creator and producer Paul Henning, told the story of the Clampett's good fortune. Recorded by Flatt and Scruggs, a bluegrass duo, it reached 44 on the charts in 1962.

Granny, Jethro, Elly May and Jed.

The original "Durwood."

BEWITCHED

ABC, 1964-1972 (306 episodes)

Theme Song: "Theme from Bewitched" by Jack Keller and Howard Greenfield

Major cast members: Elizabeth Montgomery, Dick York (1964-69), Dick Sargent (1969-1972), Agnes Moorehead, the Murphy twins (1966-1972), David White, Irene Vernon (1964-66), Kasey Rogers (1966-1972), George Tobias, Alice Pearce (1964-66), Sandra Gould (1966-1972)

The debate among "Bewitched" fans continues to this day: which Darrin do you prefer? Dick York who played the part between 1964 and 69, or Dick Sargent who took over from 1969 to 1972? Regardless of your preference, the unexplained casting change (nothing in the script commented on the rather obvious Darrin transformation) didn't adversely affect the show's high ratings. At first glance Darrin and Samantha (Elizabeth Montgomery) seemed like your average suburban couple. Darrin was an advertising executive and Samantha was a stay-at-home witch. With a wiggle of her nose she could clean the house, make supper or conjure up historical figures such as George Washington. For mild-mannered Darrin she vowed never to practice witchcraft in his presence. (It was a spin on the old sexist attitude "No wife of mine will ever work!") Of course, that was seldom ever the case. A reliable stream of solid character actors lent support to the show, including Samatha's mother Endora (Agnes Moorehead), who constantly badgered poor Darrin, or "Durwood" as she called him; and the nosy neighbors the Kravitzes (George Tobias and Alice Pearce). The Stevens couple eventually had a daughter, Tabatha (played by twins Erin and Diane Murphy), and a son, Adam. "Tabatha" was spun-off as a not-too-successful sequel to the series. The show's theme was a snappy little melody performed as an instrumental while an animated witch flew around and introduced the credits.

BONANZA

NBC, 1959-1973 (440 episodes)

Theme Song: "Bonanza" by Jay Livingston and Ray Evans

Major cast members: Lorne Greene, Michael Landon, Dan Blocker (1959-72), Pernell Roberts (1959-65), Victor Sen Yung, David Canary (1972-73), Ray Teal (1960-1972), Mitch Vogel (1970-73), Bing Russell (1961-1973)

If you weren't a fan of the Western, TV pickin's were kind of slim in the late '50s. In fact, when "Bonanza" premiered in 1959 there were 30 Westerns taking up the prime time lineup of the three networks. Originally scheduled opposite the powerhouse "Perry Mason," audiences initially preferred watching courtroom wrangling to seeing a bunch of wranglers named Cartwright. That soon changed and the weekly adventures of Ben, Little Joe, Hoss and Adam went on to become one of the most popular shows in television history. "Bonanza" took place on the vast expanse of the Ponderosa Ranch in 1850s Nevada. Set in the wild, wild west, "Bonanza" combined elements of an action/adventure series, with regular lapses into situation comedy. Most of the comedic moments were provided by the burly brother Hoss (Dan Blocker). Ben (Lorne Greene) was the patriarch of the Cartwright clan. A typical plot had Ben fighting the bad guys, bailing his grown sons (Blocker, Pernell Roberts, and Michael Landon) out of predicaments, and keeping the sibling rivalry down to a minimum. This formula kept the show on for 14 years, the second longest-running Western next to "Gunsmoke." The "Bonanza" theme, written by three-time Oscar-winners Jay Livingston and Ray Evans, made the hit parade and was actually sung on the opening show by the Cartwright men.

Little Joe, Hoss and Adam squabbling again.

THE BRADY BUNCH

ABC, 1969-1974 (117 episodes)

Theme Song: "The Brady Bunch" by Sherwood Schwartz and Frank Devol

Major cast members: Florence Henderson, Robert Reed, Ann B. Davis, Maureen McCormick, Eve Plumb, Susan Olsen, Christopher Knight, Barry Williams, Mike Lookinland

It would have been hard to imagine that this show from the late '60s and early '70s would become a major big screen box office hit in 1995! But that was the case with "The Brady Bunch Movie." It's even harder to imagine how this show could have survived during the height of the Vietnam War. Talk about escapism! We all know the story of "a man named Brady, who was busy with three boys of his own" and the "lovely lady who had three girls of her own." "The Brady Bunch" consisted of the melding of a widow (Florence Henderson) and her three daughters with a widower (Robert Reed) and his three sons. One of the last of the wholesome family sitcoms that proliferated in the '50s, the Bradys lived in a four-bedroom home (complete with an astroturf lawn) in suburban Los Angeles. The kids confronted the usual childhood problems — school, boys, girls, a bad case of acne, etc. Mom and Dad were quick to dispense just the right dose of sound advice. And the wacky housekeeper Alice (Ann B. Davis) was ready with some fresh-baked cookies. The opening theme told the story of how this mob formed a family and became "The Brady Bunch." An animated spin-off called "The Brady Kids" ran on ABC from 1972-74.

In an established TV sitcom tradition, the Brady Bunch kids had a brief recording career.

Carol.

THE CAROL BURNETT SHOW

CBS, 1967-1979 (224 episodes)

Theme Song: "I'm So Glad We Had This Time Together" by Joe Hamilton

Cast: Carol Burnett, Harvey Korman, (1967-77), Lyle Waggoner (1967-74), Vicki Lawrence (1967-79), Tim Conway (1975-79), Dick Van Dyke (1977), Kenneth Mars (1979), Craig Richard Nelson (1979)

For twelve years on CBS, Saturday night television viewers were "so glad we had this time together" with Carol Burnett. The secret to the show's longevity? Carol connected with her audience. As host of televisions's last great variety show, she broke the ice each week by taking questions from the studio audience. Then came the variety: songs, dances, guest stars, and especially slide-splitting comedy sketches, such as the always bickering Ed and Eunice ("Mama's Family" was a situation comedy spin-off from this sketch), the office hilarity of Mr. Tudball and Mrs. Wiggins, the continuing soap opera parody "As the Stomach Turns," and send-ups of classic films such as "Gone With the Wind" and "From Here To Eternity." Carol's talents as a comic actress kept things at a high pitch, and the show's hilarious resident ensemble (Harvey Korman, Vicki Lawrence, Tim Conway, Lyle Waggoner) has certainly never been surpassed in the history of the medium. In addition, nearly every episode featured finely crafted musical numbers performed by the resident company of dancers, choreographed by Ernie Flatt. Carol, with her attractive Broadway belt, was often featured in duet with a guest star in a trademark style of lengthy music medley. She always closed the show with a tug of her ear (a private greeting to her grandmother), and sang the theme song "I'm So Glad We Had This Time Together," written by producer Joe Hamilton, Carol's husband. When "The Carol Burnett Show" left the air in 1979, the variety format of television, with its roots going back to the last gasps of vaudeville, virtually died. Fortunately, Carol's shows, now in rerun syndication, never seem to age.

THE COURTSHIP OF EDDIE'S FATHER

ABC, 1969-1972 (78 episodes)

Theme Song: "Courtship of Eddie's Father" by Harry Nilsson

Major cast members: Bill Bixby, Brandon Cruz, Miyoshi Umeki, James Komack, Kristina Holland, Jodie Foster

Before it became a TV series "The Courtship of Eddie's Father" was a novel by Mark Toby and a 1963 film starring Glenn Ford, little Ronny Howard (Opie at the time, later Richie Cunningham, and who grew up to be a big film director) and Shirley Jones. Three years after Bill Bixby ended his stint on "My Favorite Martian" he was cast in the role of magazine editor Tom Corbett in "The Courtship of Eddie's Father." Brandon Cruz was cast as the young and precocious Eddie, who constantly attempted to devise ways to return his father (a widower) to the matrimonial altar. To that end, Eddie takes on the role of matchmaker and parades a bevy of beauties in front of the not-so-interested dad. The "courtship" that develops is really between dad and son as the two use each episode as an opportunity to more closely bond. In the tradition of the family sitcom, the series had many warm and humorous moments. Supporting cast members included the confused housekeeper Mrs. Livingston (Miyoshi Umeki), the ultra-hip magazine photographer (the show's executive producer, James Komack) and Eddie's friend Joey Kelly (the future film mega-star and Oscar winner Jodie Foster). Pop singer Harry Nilsson wrote and performed the show's theme song about his "best friend."

Eddie and Father.

Alex and Donna take Jeff's temperature.

THE DONNA REED SHOW

ABC, 1958-1966 (275 episodes)

Theme Song: "Donna Reed Theme" by Jack Keller and Howard Greenfield

Major cast members: Donna Reed, Carl Betz, Shelley Fabares (1958-63), Paul Petersen, Patty Petersen (1963-66), Bob Crane (1963-65), Ann McCrea (1963-66), Darryl Richard (1965-66), Kathleen Freeman, Howard McNear, Janet Langard

Donna Reed played the nice girl in "It's a Wonderful Life" and the not-so-nice girl in "From Here to Eternity." When she starred in her own show she became the model mother, the epitome of wholesome. At the center of this warm and humorous family comedy was Donna Stone (Reed), her husband Alex (Carl Betz), a pediatrician, and their active kids (Shelley Fabares and Paul Petersen). Like so many shows from those crazy, hazy, lazy '50s, this one took place in a WASPY, middle class, white bread town (Hilldale, Any State, U.S.A.). The problems of the Stone family were not unlike those of the Cleavers in "Leave It to Beaver" or the Andersons in "Father Knows Best"—measles, girlfriends and boyfriends, school problems, telling lies, etc. Donna usually kept the household in some type of order as her husband was usually off at odd hours to make house calls (remember those) and attend to his patients. The most shocking thing the kids did was to enjoy a brief fling recording hit records. Paul Petersen had a hit in 1962 with the novelty song, "She Can't Find Her Keys." That same year Shelley Fabares did even better. Her recording of "Johnny Angel" went to number one and earned her a gold record. (Neither actor wanted to make records, following the Ricky Nelson model.) She went on to star in Elvis films, and to become a television fixture in several other series, including "Coach." After Fabares' departure from the series, Paul Petersen's real-life sister, Patty, joined the cast as a newly adopted daughter of the Stone family.

The Andersons say grace over a Thanksgiving dinner of hamburgers (you'd have to see the episode to get it).

FATHER KNOWS BEST

CBS 1954-55, 1958-62 (1960-62 prime-time reruns)
NBC 1955-58

ABC (1962-63 prime-time reruns) 203 episodes

Theme Song: "Father Knows Best Theme"
by Don Ferris and Irving Friedman

Major cast members: Robert Young, Jane Wyatt, Elinor Donahue, Billy Gray, Lauren Chapin, Sarah Selby, Yvonne Lime (1954-57), Paul Wallace (1954-59), Jimmy Bates (1954-59), Robert Foulk (1955-59), Vivi Jannis (1955-59), Roger Smith (1957-58), Roberta Shore (1957-58)

An affable insurance agent named Jim Anderson (Robert Young), his steadfast wife Margaret (Jane Wyatt) and their three angelic children, nicknamed Princess (Elinor Donahue), Bud (Billy Gray) and Kitten (Lauren Chapin) lived at 607 South Maple Street in the midwestern town of Springfield. This is too perfect. How can anything go wrong in this wholesome household? On those rare occasions where there was some domestic discord, usually involving school, friends and the opposite sex, Jim would restore the family to normalcy with a warm smile, some calming words, and some mushy background scoring. As the breadwinner, Jim would return home every night, and in the style of Mr. Rogers, take off his sports jacket, slip into a comfortable sweater, and then tackle the problems of the day. It was never explained why Mom couldn't handle these problems, but she was probably too busy baking cookies. Unlike other family sitcoms of this period in which usually one or the other parent was a boob (usually the dad—this stylized convention returned in full-force in the sitcoms of the '80s and '90s), both Jim and Margaret were responsible adults. This idealized view of the American household was used as a positive model for millions of families throughout the country. During its final season, "Father Knows Best" received its highest ratings — sixth overall. In a move that was unprecedented at the time, Robert Young grew tired of the role and called it quits. He later went on to star in the popular medical series "Marcus Welby, M.D."

THE FLINTSTONES

ABC, 1960-66, (166 episodes)

Theme Song: "(Meet) The Flintstones"
by William Hanna, Joseph Barbera and Hoyt S. Curtin

Character voices: Alan Reed, Jean Vander Pyl, Mel Blanc, Bea Benaderet, Gerry Johnson

"Yabba Dabba Doo!" Created by the Hanna-Barbera animation studio, "The Flintstones" was a prehistoric takeoff inspired by "The Honeymooners." The Flintstone family lived in suburban Bedrock, where Fred worked in the local quarry with his best friend and next-door neighbor Barney Rubble. Fred's wife Wilma was a homemaker, and raised their young daughter Pebbles. Barney's wife, Betty hung around with Wilma and raised their adopted son Bamm-Bamm. Voices were supplied by Alan Reed (Fred) and Mel Blanc (the original Barney). Blanc also provided the sounds for the Flintstone's pet, Dino the dinosaur. The first cartoon to break into prime-time, "The Flintstones" appealed to adults as well as children. It was the first animated sitcom, and at its best parodied that genre and suburban life itself. Guest characters included such popular cultural icons as Ann-Margrock, Cary Granite, Stony Curtis, Perry Masonry, and TV host Ed Sullystone. "The Flintstones" continues to be a merchandising powerhouse with a line of cereal, children's vitamins and other commercial spin-offs. In 1994, a live action version of "The Flintstones" starring John Goodman as Fred hit the big screen.

Max and 99.

GET SMART

NBC, 1965-1970 (138 episodes)

Theme Song: "Get Smart" by Irving Szathmary

Major cast members: Don Adams, Barbara Feldon, Edward Platt, Bernie Kopell (1966-69), Robert Karvelas (1967-1970), Victor French, Dick Gautier (1966-69)

Would you believe "Get Smart" was the longest running sitcom in television history? Of course not. But the "would you believe . . .?" comedy schtick popularized by super agent 86 Maxwell Smart (Don Adams) in "Get Smart" became part of the '60s jargon. Smart's number 86 was also a joke: the number being bartender lingo for cutting off service to a drunk! The show, a spy spoof, was the creation of Mel Brooks and Buck Henry. Smart was teamed with Agent 99 (Barbara Feldon) as he bungled his way from one case to another. Max and 99 were part of an international spy organization known as Control, led by the perfect comic foil The Chief (Edward Platt). Using such innovative devices as a shoe phone and the Cone of Silence, Smart tried to outsmart the evil agents of KAOS, an international crime organization hellbent on taking over the world. Despite Smart's ineptitude, the spies at KAOS were even dumber. When the show began to slip in the ratings, Smart and 99 tied the knot and later had twin boys. Years after the show was cancelled, Maxwell Smart returned to the big screen in "The Naked Bomb." Other TV movies, and a short-lived new "Get Smart" series aired. None of these versions captured the consistent hilarity of the original. The show's instrumental theme accompanies the memorable opening sequence as Smart passes through a series of slamming doors before dropping down a telephone booth to the Control headquarters. One parting thought: has any TV show ever had a better title than this one?

HAZEL

NBC, 1961-65, CBS, 1966 (154 episodes)

Theme Song: "Hazel" by Howard Greenfield and Jack Keller

Major cast members: Shirley Booth, Don DeFore (1961-65), Howard Smith, Maudie Prickett, Whitney Blake (1961-65), Bobby Buntrock, Ray Fulmer (1965-66), Lynn Bordon (1965-66), Julia Benjamin (1965-66)

Based on the popular *The Saturday Evening Post* cartoon, the sitcom was about the slightly daffy maid Hazel (Academy Award-winning actress Shirley Booth). The show followed two formats during its run. In the first (1961-65), Hazel lived with the Baxters at 123 Marshall Road, Hydsberg, New York. The know-it-all Hazel constantly meddled in the affairs of the family, particularly those of the head of the household, George (Don DeFore), called "Mr. B." With her work done (and the show in need of a recharge), Hazel moved across town to the home of George's brother Steve (Ray Fulmer), a real estate broker with a wife, Barbara (Julia Benjamin) and daughter, Susie (Lynn Bordon). The reason given for the move was that George, a lawyer, had been transferred to the Middle East on business. He did hand over his son, Harold (Bobby Buntrock) to his brother because he didn't want to interrupt the kid's education. More likely, the producers wanted to retain some consistency. Whatever the reason, it didn't work. Hazel and her new family only survived one season before CBS hung up her dust cloth for good.

Hazel and the Baxters.

HOGAN'S HEROES

NBC, 1965-1971 (168 episodes)

Theme Song: "Hogan's Heroes March" by Jerry Fielding

Major cast members: Robert Crane, Werner Klemperer, John Banner, Robert Clary, Richard Dawson, Larry Hovis, Leon Askin, Ivan Dixon (1965-1970)

Can life in a World War II German POW camp be funny? For six seasons audiences thought so. That was the run of "Hogan's Heroes," a show about an enterprising American POW, Col. Robert Hogan (Bob Crane), his merry band of saboteurs, and a bunch of bumbling Germans, led by Col. Klink (Werner Klemperer) and his portly sidekick Sgt. Schultz (John Banner). A blatant rip-off of Billy Wilder's 1950 film "Stalag 17," "Hogan's" creators were in fact successfully sued for plagiarism by the authors of the play and movie. Each week Hogan would devise another way to outsmart the enemy, usually by securing top secret information from the oh-so gullable Germans, communicate to the allies with a stashed shortwave radio or guide comrades to freedom through a network of underground tunnels. The work of Hogan and his men was too important to the allied cause to actually escape. But that really didn't matter since life in Stalag 13 was more akin to a three star hotel than a prisoner-of-war camp. (Many publicly protested the show's frivolous treatment of Nazi prison camp life.) The "Heroes" included real-life POW Robert Clary and "Family Feud" kisser Richard Dawson. The show's theme, a traditional sounding military march, accompanied the opening credits which introduced viewers to the camp and its inhabitants.

Sgt. Schultz, Col. Klink and Hogan.

Buffalo Bob and Howdy Doody.

HOWDY DOODY

NBC, 1947-1950 (2,343 episodes)

Theme Song: "It's Howdy Doody Time" by Edward George Kean

Major cast members: Bob Smith, Bob Keeshan (1947-1955), Bob Nicholson, Lou Anderson

"Howdy Doody" is considered the first national breakthrough show for kids. Originally a radio program, it made its television debut in 1947. An original character on the radio show, Elmer, used to greet Buffalo Bob Smith with the words, "Well, howdy doody." A few years later the wooden freckled-faced marionette greeted Buffalo Bob the same way, but was also given the name. The show quickly expanded from three to five shows a week and the waiting list for tickets to sit in the studio audience extended for years. Wearing a fringed cowboy suit, Buffalo Bob (a native of Buffalo, N.Y.) played some songs on the piano and acted the role of the amiable host. In addition to Bob and Howdy, the other characters that inhabited Doodyville were Phineas T. Bluster (the mayor), Dilly Dally (an inept carpenter), Flub-A-Dub (an amalgamation of seven different animals), Heidi Doody (Howdy's sister), and his twin brother, Double Doody. Human characters included Chief Thunderthud (Bill "Cowabunga!" LeCornec), Princess Summerfall Winterspring (Judy Tyler) and Clarabell the Clown (Bob Keeshan). Clarabell, a seltzer-squirting clown, in the tradition of another great clown, Harpo Marx, never talked. Keeshan shed the clown costume in 1955 to star in his own successful kid's show, "Captain Kangaroo." The theme song for the show was a variation on the singable "Ta-Ra-Ra-Boom-De-Ay."

I DREAM OF JEANNIE

NBC, 1965-1970 (139 episodes)

Theme Song: "Jeannie" by Hugh Montenegro and Buddy Kaye

Major cast members: Barbara Eden, Larry Hagman, Bill Dailey, Hayden Rorke, Emmaline Henry (1966-1970), Philip Ober (1965-66), Barton MacLane (1965-69), Vinton Hayworth (1969-1970)

Long before Larry Hagman became the dastardly J. R. Ewing on the long-running prime time soap "Dallas" he played the affable and sometimes befuddled astronaut Tony Nelson for six seasons on NBC's "I Dream of Jeannie." In a plotline that would never fly in the '90s, Nelson's rocket is downed on a desert island, where he uncorks a bottle containing a well-preserved 2,000-year-old genie (Barbara Eden). Indebted for "freeing" her, Jeannie proclaims Nelson her "master." Jeannie returns to Cocoa Beach, Florida, where she sets up home with Nelson and turns his life topsy-turvey as he tries to conceal his find from his military colleagues, particularly the nosy base psychiatrist Dr. Alfred Bellows (Hayden Rorke). Only his best friend and next door neighbor, fellow astronaut Roger Healy (Bill Dailey), knows about Jeannie's magical powers. The show never made a big stir in the ratings, but the original concept to expose Jeannie's navel caused an uproar (and some decent publicity for the show) with the network censors. The solution: put a flesh-colored cloth plug in to conceal it to the"naked eye." In 1969, Major Nelson and Jeannie tied the knot. An animated version of the series ran from 1973 to 1975 and a TV movie starring Eden and Wayne Rogers (Hagman was too busy filming "Dallas") also aired. The show's opening credits, done in animation, uses the theme music to depict how Nelson first discovered his genie in the bottle.

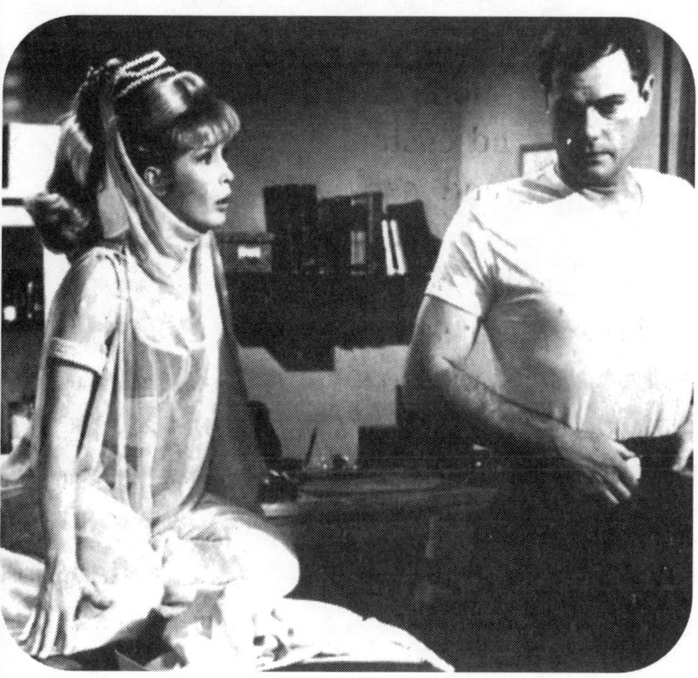

Jeannie and Tony.

Lucy and Ethel cook up another hare-brained scheme.

I LOVE LUCY

CBS, 1951-57 (179 episodes)

Theme Song: "I Love Lucy" by Harold Adamson and Eliot Daniel

Major cast members: Lucille Ball, Desi Arnaz, William Frawley, Vivian Vance, Richard Keith (1956-57), Mary Jane Croft (1957), Frank Nelson (1957)

For almost two decades Lucille Ball worked regularly in films, never achieving major star status. Her fortunes changed when she made the jump into the new-fangled industry known as television. With the debut of "I Love Lucy" in 1951, Lucille Ball became the most dominant force in television for the rest of the decade. In fact, with various other reincarnations "The Lucille Ball-Desi Arnaz Show," "The Lucy Show" and "Here's Lucy" she reined as the "queen of television" for more than two decades. Actually, the concept for "I Love Lucy" grew out of a late '40s radio program "My Favorite Husband," also starring Ball. When CBS wanted to take the concept to television, Ball agreed under two conditions: her real-life husband, actor/singer/Cuban bandleader Desi Arnaz, would play her TV husband and it would be produced by her own production company, Desilu, in Hollywood. CBS thought a Cuban husband wasn't American enough for America. (This was not, however, a politically charged decision, since Castro's revolution occurred several years after the series began.) Ball and Arnaz put together a nightclub act, toured the country, and came back to CBS with proof that the redhead-Cuban combination was an audience-pleaser. CBS capitulated. Ball and Arnaz played Lucy and Ricky Ricardo. William Frawley and Vivian Vance played their best friends and apartment neighbors, Fred and Ethel Mertz. The show was a screwball comedy (which actually is a genre that hasn't often succeeded on television), with Lucy finding a way to get into a new predicament every week, whether it was as a Vitametavegim salesman, a cake decorator, a grape-stomper in Italy, or a star-struck Hollywood visitor. As the entire world knows, Lucy was always trying to break into show business, and Ricky was always saying no. "I Love Lucy" was the first TV series to be shot on film using three cameras (a technique still used today). Between 1952 and 1957 the series never ranked below third in the ratings. The show's Latin rhythm theme is among the most memorable in TV history and still enjoys some play as a jazz instrumental. The seldom heard lyrics were actually sung on an episode by Arnaz.

Jack Benny, forever 39.

THE JACK BENNY SHOW

CBS, 1950-1964 (304 episodes)

NBC, 1964-65 (39 episodes)

Theme Song: "Love In Bloom" by Leo Robin and Ralph Rainger

Major cast members: Jack Benny, Mary Livingstone, Eddie "Rochester" Anderson, Dennis Day, Don Wilson, Mel Blanc, Frank Nelson

Sort of a cross between a sitcom and a variety show, "The Jack Benny Show" was a successful transplant from radio. His persona etched after years in vaudeville and radio, Benny brought his familiar brand of schtick to the small screen. This included his life-long insistence that he was only 39, and his stinginess as evidenced by his driving a 1928 Maxwell (that's a car). An acknowledged master of comic timing, Benny could illicit a laugh with a simple hand gesture or the way he said such familiar phrases as "Well . . .," "Wait a minute!" and "Now cut that out!" Then there was his violin playing that sounded like fingernails rubbing on a blackboard. It was all part of the comic character, since Benny was actually a competent violinist. Never egocentric, Benny often let his ensemble cast have the best laugh lines. These people included Eddie "Rochester" Anderson as his valet, announcer Don Wilson, Mel Blanc, who played a variety of roles and Benny's real-life wife, Mary Livingstone. Benny's theme, "Love in Bloom" was written for the 1934 Bing Crosby film *She Loves Me Not*. One night when Mr. and Mrs. Benny were visiting a nightclub, the bandleader asked Benny to join him at the violin in the next number, which was "Love in Bloom." A newspaper columnist wrote about the impromptu performance and soon Benny couldn't enter a nightclub without the band striking up the song. Figuring he had a good thing going, he adapted it as his theme song.

THE JETSONS

ABC, 1962 (24 episodes)

Theme Song: "Jetsons Main Theme" by William Hanna, Joseph Barbera and Hoyt Curtin

Character voices: George O'Hanlon, Penny Singleton, Janet Waldo, Daws Butler, Mel Blanc, Don Messick, Jean Vander Pyl

"The Flintstones" was an animated sitcom set in the Stone Age. The creators at Hanna-Barbera took this winning formula and updated it to the space age and called it "The Jetsons." Also animated, this was another typical family show set in suburbia. As the theme song goes: "Meet George Jetson" — a computer digital index operator at Spacely Space Age Sprockets; "Jane, his wife" — the happy homemaker who takes care of the two kids, Jane and Elroy in their comfortable Skypad Apartment. The family wouldn't be complete without Astro (or rather Rrr-Astro), the dog, or their robot housekeeper, Rosie. Celebrity voices included "Blondie" star Penny Singleton as Jane and Mel Blanc as George's boss, the tyrannical Mr. Spacely. One season of 24 episodes was made and repeated from 1963 to 1983. In 1984, 41 new shows were added, and in 1987 an additional 10, enough to assure another long run in syndication. In the '90s, a feature-length film was made. A footnote in TV history, "The Jetsons" was the first color program to air on ABC. As for the show's theme, not much of a melody, but almost everybody seems to be able to recite the words.

The amazing Lassie and original cast.

LASSIE

CBS, 1954-1971

Theme Song: "The Secret of Silent Hills" by William Lava and Charles Newman

Major cast members: Tommy Rettig (1954-57), Jan Clayton (1954-57), George Cleveland (1954-57), Jon Provost (1957-1964), Cloris Leachman (1957-58), June Lockhart (1958-1964), John Shepodd (1957-58), Hugh Reilly (1958-1964), Larry Wilcox (1972-74)

This show had legs — four to be exact. It also ran for 17 years. Inspired by Eric Knight's best-selling 1940 novel, *Lassie Come Home* and the 1943 film version starring a little known child actress named Elizabeth Taylor, "Lassie" went on to become a children's programming mainstay. During the program's run, no less than six male collies trained and owned by Rudd Weatherwax starred as the female pooch. Through the years the cast featured such two-footed members as Tommy Rettig, Jan Clayton, Jon Provost, June Lockhart and Cloris Leachman. The human cast usually took a back seat to the canine — the one constant throughout the run of the series. Lassie, a brave, loyal and intelligent dog, was able to change her allegiance with apparent ease. For the first 10 years of the series Lassie lived on a farm with a small boy; for the next four years she lived with a forest ranger; and finally Lassie was on her own. Somehow, Lassie never seemed to be confused by all these casting changes. The show was revived in 1973 as an animated series and returned again in the '80s as "The New Lassie." The early '90s also saw a new feature length film version of "Lassie."

LEAVE IT TO BEAVER

CBS, 1957-58, ABC, 1958-1963 (234 episodes)

Theme Song: "The Toy Parade" by D. Kahn, M. Lenard, M. Greene

Major cast members: Barbara Billingsley, Hugh Beaumont, Jerry Mathers, Tony Dow, Ken Osmond, Diane Brewster (1957-58), Sue Randall (1958-1962), Rusty Stevens (1958-1960), Stanley Fafara, Richard Deacon

Talk about the show that refuses to die, this has to be it. "Leave It to Beaver" never broke the top 25 in the ratings, yet in rerun syndication it flourished (much like "Star Trek"). In fact, more than 30 years after the original show aired, "new" episodes were filmed for first-run syndication featuring a middle-aged Beaver, Wally, Eddie and an elderly June. The oh-so-wholesome Cleaver family, Theodore, inexplicably nicknamed "the Beaver" (Jerry Mathers), his older brother Wally (Tony Dow) and parents June (Barbara Billingsley) and Ward (Hugh Beaumont) lived in the middle class neighborhood of Mayfield, U.S.A. What could possibly go wrong here? Beaver's seemingly tame (by today's standards) predicaments could be solved with a few wise words from Dad, usually in the last five minutes of the episode, with a slow strings version of the theme music in the background. For those bigger problems, say girls, for example, "the Beav" could always turn to his older and more experienced brother Wally. Beaver and Wally hung around with their pals, Lumpy, Larry and Whitey. Perhaps the most interesting character on the show was Eddie Haskell (Ken Osmond), Wally's sneaky and obnoxious friend. (Even June was on to Eddie.) Years later, Osmond wore a badge for the L.A.P.D. Probably the last cop you'd ever want to be pulled over by! When the new syndicated series came up, Osmond shed the police blues and effortlessly slipped back into the role of the now middle-aged but still obnoxious Eddie. Along the lines of other '50s sitcoms, most notably "Father Knows Best" and "The Donna Reed Show," "Beaver" was a show about normal kids and perfect parents.

Wally and the Beav.

THE LIFE AND LEGEND OF WYATT EARP

ABC, 1955-1961 (266 episodes)

Theme Song: "The Life and Legend of Wyatt Earp" by Harry Warren and Harold Adamson

Major cast members: Hugh O'Brien, Morgan Woodward (1958-1961), Douglas Fowley (1955-1961), Steve Brodie (1959-1961), Mason Dinehart III (1955-57), Damian O'Flynn (1959-1961), Trevor Bardette (1959-1961), William Tannen (1957-58), Denver Pyle (1955-56)

Before "Bonanza" and "Gunsmoke" there was "Wyatt Earp." Considered TV's first "adult" western, the righteous U.S. Marshall Earp was played convincingly by Hugh O'Brien. Part of the show's realism can be attributed to the fact that Arthur Lake (no, not the guy who played Dagwood), who had lived with Earp for the last four years of his life, acted as a technical advisor on the program. The final episode (built up over a five-part story) culminated in Earp's most famous moment — the gunfight at the OK Corral. The show's theme has a special significance because it was written by one of the true giants of the American popular song — Harry Warren, a three-time Oscar winner who wrote such classics as "We're in the Money," "42nd Street," "You'll Never Know," "Jeepers Creepers," "Chattanooga Choo Choo" and dozens of other song standards.

THE LONE RANGER

ABC, 1949-1957 (221 episodes)

Theme Song: "William Tell Overture" by Giachino Rossini; the opera was composed in 1829

Major cast members: Clayton Moore (1949-1952, 1954-57), John Hart (1952-54), Jay Silverheels

"Hi-yo Silver, away!" And with those words the Lone Ranger (Clayton Moore) and his trusted friend Tonto (Jay Silverheels) went in hot pursuit of the bad guys. One of the first Westerns to hit the new-fangled phenomenon known as television, "The Lone Ranger", which originated on radio in 1933, was typical of the early examples of the genre: simple plot, minimal character development and white hats versus black hats. One of six Texas rangers to be seriously injured in an ambush, John Reid was nursed back to health by Tonto, a native American whom Reid had once helped. They decided to team up and avenge all the wrongs taking place in the wild, wild west, but first, Reid donned a mask to protect his identity and became the Lone Ranger. Do you follow the storyline, kemo sabe? Parents loved the show because the Lone Ranger never had to kill anyone and for a man of the old west he used perfect grammar—a good influence on those young folk. "The Lone Ranger" later aired as a Saturday morning animated series and Moore played the masked man in two feature films made in the late '50s.

The second Thomas TV family.

MAKE ROOM FOR DADDY/ THE DANNY THOMAS SHOW

ABC, 1953-57, CBS, 1957-1964 (336 episodes)

Theme Song: "Danny Boy" ("Londonderry Air") Irish traditional melody with lyrics by Fred Weatherly

Major cast members: (format one, 1953-57): Danny Thomas, Jean Hagen, Sherry Jackson, Rusty Hammer, Amanda Randolph, Jesse White, Mary Wickes; (format two, 1957-64): Danny Thomas, Marjorie Lord, Sherry Jackson, Penny Parker, Rusty Hammer, Lelani Sorenson, Angela Cartwright, Amanda Randolph, Mary Wickes, Pat Carroll, Sheldon Leonard, Hans Conreid, Pat Harrington Jr., Annette Funicello, Bill Dana, Gale Gordon, William Demarest

The show started out as "Make Room For Daddy," but was changed to "The Danny Thomas Show" when the series moved from ABC to CBS in 1957. What makes this show historically significant is that it was the first sitcom where the father wasn't a stupid buffoon. In fact, Danny Thomas' portrayal of nightclub entertainer Danny Williams was warm and realistic. Danny was a star by night who was brought down to the real-life realities of raising a family from the moment he stepped into the door. On the strength of Thomas alone, the show managed to survive several major cast changes, most notably the departure of his on-screen wife Jean Hagen after three seasons. Hagen, the squeaky-voiced co-star of the classic film "Singin' in the Rain," called it quits after she described her part as "thankless." Since divorce was a television taboo, the writers killed off Hagen and replaced her with Majorie Lord. Throughout the run of the show, there was a memorable parade of characters, including everyone's favorite Uncle Tonoose (Hans Conreid) and such stellar sitcom regulars as Gale Gordon ("The Lucy Show," "Here's Lucy") and William Demarest ("My Three Sons"). "The Danny Thomas Show" also has the distinction of spawning the first TV spin-off. While driving on a trip, Danny was accidently caught speeding in a small southern town — Mayberry. He was pulled over by Sheriff Andy Taylor, who was soon given his own show, "The Andy Griffith Show."

MANNIX

CBS, 1967-1975 (194 episodes)

Theme Song: "Mannix" by Lalo Schifrin

Major cast members: Mike Connors, Joseph Campanella (1967-68), Gail Fisher (1968-1975), Robert Reed (1969-1975)

"Mannix" may seem tame by today's standards (consider "NYPD Blue"), but in its day it was considered shockingly violent. In fact, no episode was complete without an all-out brawl that usually resulted in an appallingly high body count. The man who preferred to let his fists do the talking was private detective Joe Mannix (Mike Connors). For the first season, Mannix was employed by a high tech detective firm called Intertect. But he didn't need computers and other fancy gadgets to do the job when his fists would do just fine, so he started his own agency (on the first floor of the building in which he lived), and hired an office assistant, Peggy Fair (Gail Fisher). Her husband, a friend of Mannix's and a former policeman, had been killed on duty. Lt. Adam Tobias (Robert Reed from "The Brady Bunch") joined the cast in 1969 and played Mannix's friend and police contact. "Mannix" was a ratings winner and proved that there was certainly an audience for violence on the tube. Radio comics Bob and Ray ran an on-going parody on the series called "Blimmix," in which the hero engaged the suspect in a polite conversation before beating him to a pulp. The jazzy theme music was fast-paced, just like the show.

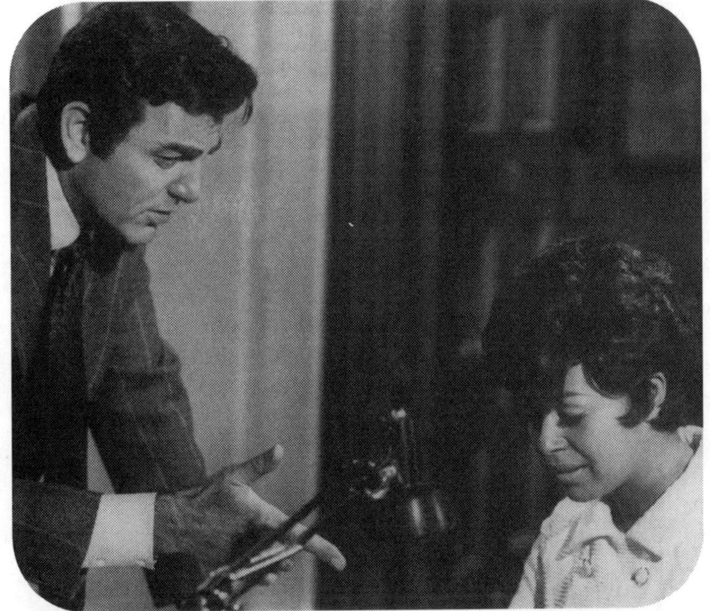

Joe Mannix and Peggy.

Maynard and Dobie.

THE MANY LOVES OF DOBIE GILLIS

CBS, 1959-1963 (147 episodes)

Theme Song: "Dobie" by Max Shulman and Lionel Newman

Major cast members: Dwayne Hickman, Bob Denver, Frank Faylen, Florida Friebus, Sheila James, Tuesday Weld (1959-1960), Warren Beatty (1959-1960), William Schallert

Based on a popular novel by Max Shulman, "The Many Loves of Dobie Gillis" focused on Dobie (Dwayne Hickman), a son of a grocer, who was struggling with the usual set of challenges all teenagers confront: girls, cars, college, money, parents, finding a job. He frequently pondered life's problems in the local park sitting underneath the statute of Rodin's *The Thinker*, even imitating the statue's crouching position. His best friend, Maynard G. Krebs (played by TV's future "Gilligan," Bob Denver), was television's first regular beatnik, complete with dingy sweatshirt, baggy pants and a little goatee. Krebs was so laid back just the thought of work would send him into convulsions. Dobie's "main squeeze," Thalia (Tuesday Weld), was an attractive gold-digger who wanted "her man" to provide her with all of life's creature comforts. Zelda, a brainy female nerd, was Dobie's platonic confidant. Another teenager in the show, Dobie's rival for Thalia's affections, was a handsome young actor, who was quickly pulled from the cast when his handlers determined he was destined for a big career in feature films. His name: Warren Beatty. During the show's run, Dobie went from high school into the army and finally to college. Unlike other shows of this period such as "Father Knows Best" and "Leave It to Beaver," "The Many Loves of Dobie Gillis" was more realistic, depicting everyday kids with real everyday problems. A few reunion versions of the program aired in the '80s.

McHALE'S NAVY

ABC, 1962-66 (138 episodes)

Theme Song: "McHale's Navy March" by Alex Stordahl

Major cast members: Ernest Borgnine, Tim Conway, Joe Flynn, Bob Hastings, Gavin MacLeod, Edson Stroll, Gary Vinson, John Wright, Carl Ballantine, Yoshio Yoda

Considered a nautical version of "The Phil Silvers Show," "McHale's Navy" took place on the fictional South Pacific island of Taratupa during World War II. Lieutenant Commander Quinton McHale (Oscar-winner Ernest Borgnine) commanded a group of rowdy sailors who were assigned to PT73. These sailors (including Gavin MacLeod before "The Mary Tyler Moore Show" and his own nautical series "The Love Boat") were more interested in women and partying than fighting the Japanese. McHale and his men were constantly at odds with the base's commanding officer Captain Wallace Binghamton (Joe Flynn), also known as "Old Lead Bottom." Binghamton had one mission: find McHale and his men in the act of screwing up so he could court martial McHale and his "pirates" and rid them from the base. Of course, he always failed. During the last year of the series, the show moved to the European theater as McHale and the rest of the cast fought the war from Voltafiore, a small town in southern Italy. Tim Conway played McHale's executive officer, the bumbling Ensign Parker, and Bob Hastings was equally inept as Binghamton's assistant Lieutenant Carpenter. The show's instrumental theme was played during the opening credits as PT73 churns through the water.

McHale (center) and the finest in the fleet.

Jimmie and Mouseketeers.

THE MICKEY MOUSE CLUB

ABC/Syndicated, 1955-59/still in syndication (390 episodes, 1955-59)

Theme Song: "Mickey Mouse March" by Jimmie Dodd

Host: Jimmie Dodd; Co-host: Roy Williams; Selected Mouseketeers: Annette Funicello, Darlene Gillespie, Carl "Cubby" O'Brien, Karen Pendleton, Tommy Cole, Bobby Burgess, Johnny Crawford, Lonnie Burr, Don Grady, Doreen Tracey, Cheryl Holdridge, Paul Petersen

"Who's the leader of the club that's made for you and me? M-I-C-K-E-Y M-O-U-S-E." And with those familiar words, Walt Disney launched a television extravaganza. "The Mickey Mouse Club" featured more than 40 kids, or rather Mouseketeers, who donned mouse ears during the four-year run of this show. Originally, more than 3,000 children auditioned for a chance to be on the program. Hosted by Jimmie Dodd (who also penned the theme song), and "the Big Mouseketeer," Roy Williams, each episode included music, songs, dances, cartoons and adventure serials. Among the most popular: "The Adventures of Spin and Marty," "The Hardy Boys," "Annette" and "Corky and White Shadow." Kids couldn't wait to get home from school to share some precious moments with their extended family — the Mouseketeers. A few, such as Annette Funicello, were able to shed their mouse ears and pursue a career beyond "The Mickey Mouse Club." In Annette's case, she joined Frankie Avalon in a series of light and frothy "beach blanket" movies. Another Mouseketeer, Bobby Burgess, went on to dance on the Lawrence Welk Show, and Don Grady, Robbie on "My Three Sons," was also a Mouseketeer in his young days.

MISSION: IMPOSSIBLE

CBS, 1966-1973 (171 episodes)

Theme Song: "Mission: Impossible Theme" by Lalo Schifrin

Major cast members: Peter Graves (1967-1973), Steve Hill (1966-67), Barbara Bain (1966-69), Martin Landau (1966-69), Greg Morris, Peter Lupus, Leonard Nimoy (1969-1971), Lynda Day George (1971-73), Sam Elliot (1970-71), Lesley Ann Warren (1970-71)

Each episode of this adventure spy series opened with Impossible Mission Force (IMF) leader Jim Phelps (Peter Graves) receiving his marching orders in a tape recorded message. The voice on the tape supplied background information, an envelope of photos and concluded with the words: "Your mission, Jim, should you decide to accept it, is . . . As always, should you or any member of your IM Force be caught or killed, the secretary will disavow any knowledge of your actions. This tape will self-destruct in five seconds." Phelps and his associates never refused an offer to topple a communist regime or stymie an organized crime caper. But before he could take on the forces of evil in an elaborately conceived "sting" type operation, he enlisted the help of his fellow IMF members. They included Cinnamon Carter (Barbara Bain), Rollin Hand (Martin Landau), Barney Collier (Greg Morris), Willy Armitage (Peter Lupus) and Paris (Leonard Nimoy *sans* pointed ears). The show was revived (again with Graves) from 1988-1990. A big screen version of "Mission: Impossible" starring Tom Cruise was made in the 1990s. The theme music was released as a single and was on *Billboard's* "Hot 100" chart for 14 weeks in 1968.

The original cast (clockwise from top left): Greg Morris, Peter Lupus, Peter Graves, Barbara Bain, Martin Landau.

Ed and Wilbur.

MISTER ED

CBS, 1961-65 (143 episodes)

Theme Song: "Mister Ed" by Jay Livingston and Ray Evans

Major cast members: Alan Young, Connie Hines, Larry Keating (1961-63), Edna Skinner (1961-64), Leon Ames (1963-65), Florence MacMichael (1963-65), Allan "Rocky" Lane (as the voice of Mister Ed)

"Mister Ed" is a case where the theme song is probably more memorable than the show itself. Written by three-time Academy Award-winning songwriters Jay Livingston (who also provides the vocals for the theme) and Ray Evans, the song tells the story of Ed, the talking horse, of course, of course. The duo was relegated to writing TV show themes (they also did "Bonanza") when the services of popular songwriters were no longer needed in films. The show itself "borrowed" its concept from the series of Francis the talking mule movies. Francis became Ed and the mule's buddy played by Donald O'Connor in the films became Alan Young on television. Wilbur Post (Young) and his wife Carol (Connie Hines) move to the country to rid themselves of the grind of the city. To Wilbur's surprise, he finds a palomino named Ed in the barn. When Wilbur was brushing down his new nag, Ed decided to talk. According to the horse's mouth, he had never talked before because he had never found anyone worth talking to, until Wilbur came along. The confusion caused by a talking horse and the predicaments Ed got Wilbur into formed the basis of the weekly plots. Although the concept was not particularly original, "Mister Ed" was the first non-animated TV show to feature a talking animal.

The lovable Fred Rogers.

MISTER ROGERS' NEIGHBORHOOD

PBS, (1967-1975) (1979-present)

Theme Song: "Won't You Be My Neighbor?" ("It's a Beautiful Day in This Neighborhood") by Fred Rogers

Major cast member: Fred Rogers

Even if you've never seen "Mister Rogers' Neighborhood" you're probably familiar with the opening theme. It has been parodied by a number of comedians, most notably Johnny Carson and Eddie Murphy. A congenial middle-aged man, Fred Rogers enters a homey set singing "It's a beautiful day in the neighborhood." While still in mid-verse he slips into a cardigan sweater and comfortable sneakers. The mastermind of this, the longest-running children's show in television history, is Fred Rogers. A former Presbyterian minister from Pittsburgh, Rogers uses stories, songs (most of which he writes, including the opening theme) and puppets to teach kids valuable life lessons. He hosted NBC's "The Children's Corner" and "Mister Rogers' Neighborhood" on Canadian TV. In 1967 he started on PBS in pretty much the same show that continues to this day. Everything about this show is comforting, including his friends such as Mr. McFeely, "the Speedy Delivery Man." Kids learn things by traveling on a toy trolley and visiting such places as a candy factory, violin shop or a zoo.

THE MONKEES

NBC, 1966-68 (58 episodes)

Theme Song: "Theme from The Monkees" by Tommy Boyce and Bobby Hart

Major cast members: David Jones, Peter Tork, Mickey Dolenz, Mike Nesmith

Irreverent, crazy, nonsensical. All those words could be used to describe "The Monkees." Inspired by the Beatles' "A Hard Day's Night," this rock 'n' roll sitcom starred Davy Jones, Michael Nesmith, Mickey Dolenz and Peter Tork as the zany rock/pop foursome known as "The Monkees." This manufactured group was the brainchild of music promoter Don Kirshner, who picked the boys from some 500 applicants. Only Tork and Nesmith had any real musical training. Jones didn't need any. He was British and cute and the girls went wild over him, the hottest teen idol of the time. Professional musicians dubbed for the four, and the music was carefully manufactured in the studio. The series looked like a forerunner to MTV music videos: slow and fast motion (borrowing ideas from silent films), distorted focus, quick cuts. The plot usually found the boys meeting up with some crooks or a damsel in distress and after the obligatory fast motion chase scene, saving the day. During its brief run, the program successfully exploited the youth market. During the run of the series "The Monkees" had several bonafide hits, including "I'm a Believer," "Last Train to Clarksville" and "Words." For a short period, the very young even forgot about The Beatles. In 1987, trying to capitalize on the nostalgia craze, "The New Monkees" was filmed for syndication. With a whole new cast, the music faded after only 13 episodes. Years later, in an attempt to capitalize on audience interest in nostalgia, three members of the original Monkees appeared at concert venues around the country with a "best of" performance. Michael Nesmith, who had tried a solo recording career in the post-Monkees years, declined to appear in the reunion act.

TV sitcom meets Rock/Pop.

Herman examined by his regular physician, Paul Lynde.

THE MUNSTERS

CBS, 1964-66 (70 episodes)

Theme Song: "The Munsters Theme" by Jack Marshall

Major cast members: Fred Gwynne, Yvonne DeCarlo, Al Lewis, Beverly Owen (1964), Pat Priest (1964-66), Butch Patrick, John Carradine, Chett Stratton, Paul Lynde

Who can forget those opening credits with that minor-keyed '60s rock 'n' roll beat theme music (dig that organ!) as Herman Munster (Fred Gwynne) bursts through the door and the supporting cast follows through the silhouette opening! Herman, a kind-hearted Frankenstein look-a-like, complete with bolts in his neck, headed the Munster home at 1313 Mockingbird Lane. Its other inhabitants included his vampire wife Lily (B-movie queen Yvonne DeCarlo), her father, Count Dracula or just plain Grandpa (Al Lewis), their werewolf son, Eddie (Butch Patrick), and their attractive and "normal" young niece, Marilyn (Beverly Owen, later Pat Priest). Marilyn was considered the family's black sheep. Herman was employed as — what else — a funeral director. Like its prime-time counterpart, "The Addams Family," the Munsters perceived their lives as the epitome of normalcy. It was the rest of society that was strangely out of sync. This reversal formed the premise of most of the episodes. More than 20 years after the original was cancelled, "The Munsters Today," featuring a whole new cast (John Schuck as Herman and Lee Meriwether as Lily) ran for three years in syndication.

THE ODD COUPLE

ABC, 1970-75 (114 episodes)

Theme Song: "The Odd Couple" by Sammy Cahn and Neal Hefti

Major cast members: Tony Randall, Jack Klugman, Al Molinaro, Gary Walberg (1970-74), Larry Gelman, Ryan MacDonald (1970-71), Joan Hotchkiss (1970-72), Elinor Donahue (1972-74)

Start out with two childhood friends. Add two divorces. One guy is a slob. The other is a hygiene freak. Put this oil and vinegar combination together as roommates and you have the makings of "The Odd Couple." The genesis of the show was a stage play by Neil Simon and then a film starring Jack Lemmon and Walter Matthau. In the New York-set TV show, Tony Randall played the part of Felix Unger, a professional photographer cum neatness fanatic, and Jack Klugman played Oscar Madison, sportswriter and boor par excellence. As the announcer asked on the opening credits, "Can two divorced men share an apartment without driving each other crazy?" The answer was obviously no and it was this domestic discord that provided the premise for the sitcom. Never a ratings winner, "The Odd Couple" has endured in rerun syndication. Randall and Madison have reprised their roles on several occasions in the stage version. Surprisingly, the first choices to play Unger and Madison were not Randall and Klugman, but rather Martin Balsam and Art Carney. The program's theme music was retained from the movie and featured lyrics (which you've probably never heard) by four-time Oscar-winner Sammy Cahn. In 1982, "The New Odd Couple" returned with a little different perspective by casting African-American actors Ron Glass and Demond Wilson as Felix and Oscar respectively. The show ran one season on ABC.

Klugman and Randall.

THE PARTRIDGE FAMILY

ABC, 1970-1974 (96 episodes)

Theme Song: "Come on Get Happy"
by Wes Farrell and Danny Janssen

Major cast members: Shirley Jones, David Cassidy, Susan Dey, Danny Bonaduce, Suzanne Crough, Jeremy Gelbwaks (1970-71), Brian Forster (1971-74), David Madden

Oscar-winner Shirley Jones left her movie career to star with her stepson, David Cassidy, in this situation comedy about a single parent family who makes it big in the music business. In the show's fictional story, the road to stardom for the Partridge family really happened by accident. Shirley Partridge (Jones) was just an average suburban widow trying to raise her young family when the kids urged her to take part in a recording session in the garage. The song they recorded, "I Think I Love You" put the Partridges on the charts, both on the show and in real life where the recording sold about four million copies. The family hit the road in their psychedelic bus and played to packed houses of pre-pubescents around the country. Besides Shirley and Keith (Cassidy), the family included Laurie (Susan Dey), Danny (Danny Bonaduce), Tracy (Suzanne Crough) and Jeremy (played by both Jeremy Gelbwaks and Brian Forster). Reubin Kinkaid (David Madden) was their fast talking, sarcastic agent. With the exception of Jones and Cassidy supplying the vocals, the rest of the family were dubbed (with studio musicians handling their instrumentals). Cassidy became a major idol of the preteen set and was mobbed at every personal appearance at the time. An animated version of "The Partridge Family" ran on ABC from 1974-75.

David Cassidy, Danny Bonaduce, Susan Dey, Shirley Jones, Suzanne Crough, Brian Forster (clockwise from top left).

Burr as Mason.

PERRY MASON

CBS, 1957-1966 (271 episodes)

Theme Song: "Perry Mason Theme" by Fred Steiner

Major cast members: Raymond Burr, Barbara Hale, William Hopper, Ray Collins (1957-65), William Talman

If the "Perry Mason" episodes had an air of realism about them, it's because the show was created by lawyer-turned-writer Erle Stanley Gardner. The character was first created for his novels, then transferred to a radio series from 1943 to 1955. Gardner personally picked the burly actor Raymond Burr to play defense attorney Mason in the TV series. Until that time, Burr had established himself as a "heavy" in a number of feature films, including Alfred Hitchcock's *Rear Window*. Mason had an enviable courtroom win-loss record of 271 to 1. This string of victories never deterred district attorney Hamilton Burger (William Talman) from passionately presenting his case. Mason's masterful courtroom technique included cross-examinations which usually caused the guilty party to breakdown and confess. Mason would unravel the secrets to the case at the end of each show by casually explaining it all to his own staff of private investigators, Paul Drake (William Hopper) and Della Street (Barbara Hale). Burr would parlay his newfound good guy image several years later in the series "Ironside" as well as in a successful string of made-for-TV "Perry Mason" films. "Perry Mason" was television's defining courtroom series until "L.A. Law" came around in the 1980s.

THE REAL McCOYS

ABC, 1957-1962, CBS, 1962-63 (224 episodes)

Theme Song: "The Real McCoys" by Harry Ruby

Major cast members: Walter Brennan, Richard Crenna, Kathleen Nolan (1957-1962), Lydia Reed, Michael Winkleman (1957-1962), Tony Martinez

Walter Brennan, perhaps the most honored character actor in film history with three best supporting actor Oscars under his belt, reluctantly switched to the small screen and enjoyed a six-year run as the cantankerous Grandpa Amos McCoy on "The Real McCoys." The original "hillbilly" sitcom didn't poke fun of countrified living as "The Beverly Hillbillies" did a few years later. In fact, "The Real McCoys" presented a humorous and believable look at country living. Grandpa Amos was the patriarch of the McCoy family. An incorrigible old codger, he could sometimes be as ornery and opinionated as Archie Bunker. That's when his grandchildren, Luke (Richard Crenna) and Hassie (Lydia Reed) and Little Luke (Michael Winkleman) and Luke's wife Kate (Kathleen Nolan) stepped in. An example of dialogue— Kate: "But Grandpa, they're two sides to everything." Amos: "Yeah, and I'm on the right side!" Although most people never admitted watching the show, the ratings said otherwise. The show ranked in the top 25 in four out of its six-year run. When the show moved to CBS in 1962, Luke became a widower and many of the plots concerned Grandpa's attempts to find him a bride. Still a ratings powerhouse, CBS unexpectedly canceled the "The Real McCoys" just as it was scheduled to be the lead-in for a new network sitcom — "The Beverly Hillbillies." The theme was written in a country style by veteran tunesmith Harry Ruby who co-wrote "Who's Sorry Now," among other hits. The lyrics were pure sitcom: "Want you to meet the family/Known as the Real McCoys . . ."

Richard Crenna, Walter Brennan, Kathleen Nolan.

ROCKY & BULLWINKLE

ABC, 1959-1961 (52 episodes)

Theme Song: "Rocky & Bullwinkle" by Frank Comstock

Major character voices: Bill Scott, June Foray, Paul Frees, Charles Ruggles, Hans Conreid, Walter Tetley, Edward Everett Horton, William Conrad (narrator)

The animated show starred Rocky, a squirrel, and Bullwinkle, a moose, who fought an on-going battle with stereotyped cold-war villains Mr Big, Boris Badenov and Natasha in, of all places, Frostbite Falls, Minnesota. It was really pretty clever satire and appealed to both children and adults. In addition to these adventures, the show featured other regular segments, including "Fractured Fairy Tales," "Peabody's Improbably History" (in which Peabody the dog traveled back through time with his adopted son, Sherman), "Adventures of Dudley Do-Right" (a heroic mountie who battled the evil Snidley Whiplash), "Aesop and Son" (which featured an unusual spin on popular fables), and "Bullwinkle's Corner" (words of wisdom from everyone's favorite moose). "Rocky & His Friends" was later renamed "The Bullwinkle Show" and ran on both NBC and ABC from 1961 to 1973.

THE ROY ROGERS SHOW

NBC, 1951-57 (101 episodes)

Theme Song: "Happy Trails" by Dale Evans

Major cast members: Roy Rogers, Dale Evans, Pat Brady, Harry Lauter

Talk about reinventing yourself! Take some squinty-eyed guy named Leonard Slye from Cincinnati, move him to California and make him a part of the Sons of the Pioneers singing group. The result: Roy Rogers, "King of the Cowboys." Rogers managed to parlay this "aw-shucks" nice guy cowboy persona into a successful string of B-Westerns, a recording career and a television series. In the series, Roy kept the peace around the ol' Double R Bar Ranch outside of Mineral City riding with his trusty horse Trigger. Roy couldn't rid the territory of those low-down rustlers and other assorted bad guys without a supporting cast that included his wife, Dale Evans (the "Queen of the West"), riding atop her horse Buttermilk, his trusty canine Bullet, and devoted ranch hand and sidekick Pat Brady, in his jeep, Nellybelle. You could say that kid from Cincinnati finally earned his spurs! Reruns of the series appeared on CBS' Saturday morning lineup from 1961-64. The show's theme was written by Dale Evans and sung at the end of every episode by Roy and Dale on horseback: "Happy trails to you until we meet again."

Maharis and Milner.

ROUTE 66

CBS, 1960-64 (116 episodes)

Theme Song: "Theme from Route 66" by Nelson Riddle

Major cast members: Martin Milner, George Maharis (1960-63), Glen Corbett (1963-64)

This was a show about two guys who "got their kicks on Route 66." The two guys, Tod Stiles (Martin Milner, who later starred in "Adam 12") and Buz Murdock (George Maharis), were opposites. Stiles was a young man with a privileged upbringing and an Ivy League education, while Maharis was from the school of hard knocks, raised in New York's Hell's Kitchen. So what brought them together? A 1960 Corvette and the allure of tooling around the country on the open road. The series was filmed on location throughout the winding roads of Route 66. Although the writing was tight and the acting solid, the plots weren't always compelling. "Route 66" was more like a weekly travelogue with Stiles and Murdock aimlessly cruising the open road, crossing paths with strangers, and meeting up with a variety of situations: romantic, suspenseful, comedic, etc. In 1962, Maharis left the series because of a lingering bout of hepatitis. He was replaced by Linc Case (Glen Corbett), a Vietnam hero from Houston, who then became Stiles' traveling partner. After 116 episodes the show finally ran out of gas. Years later the famed cross-country Route 66 (the actual road, not the show) was replaced by an interstate highway. Nelson Riddle wrote and recorded the jazzy, up-tempo theme music, which hit the charts in 1962, and was later successfully recorded by The Manhattan Transfer.

77 SUNSET STRIP

ABC, 1958-1964 (205 episodes)

Theme Song: "77 Sunset Strip" by Mack David and Jerry Livingston

Major cast members: Efrem Zimbalist, Jr., Roger Smith (1958-1963), Edd Byrnes (1958-1963), Louis Quinn (1958-1963), Jacqueline Beer (1958-63), Byron Keith (1958-1963), Richard Long (1960-61), Robert Logan (1961-63), Joan Staley (1963-64)

Man, this show was pretty much the hippest thing to hit television! "77 Sunset Strip" and its finger-snapping hit song came from the address of the two coolest private detectives, Stuart Bailey (Efrem Zimbalist Jr., who years later continued to bust the bad guys in "The FBI") and Jeff Spencer (Roger Smith, who later married Ann-Margret). Bailey had quite the resume, with an Ivy League Ph.D. As a former OSS officer, he wanted to become a college professor but became a private investigator instead. Spencer, who had a law degree, was also a former government spy. Oh yes, and both of them were judo experts. Although Hollywood was their base, they traveled the world on various cases. Next door to number 77 was Dino's, a posh restaurant with a not-so-posh parking lot attendant, Gerald Lloyd Kookson III, better known as Kookie (Edd Byrnes). The gangly and jive-talking Kookie eventually stole the show. A forerunner to "Happy Day's" Fonzie, Kookie had the youth of this nation speaking in "kookie-isms." Some examples: "the ginchiest" (the greatest), "piling up the Z's" (sleeping), "keep the eyeballs rolling" (be on the lookout), and "a dark seven" (a bad week). Kookie not only provided comic relief, he also assisted Bailey and Spencer in their crime fighting efforts. He, along with Connie Stevens, also recorded a hit song "Kookie, Kookie, Lend Me Your Comb." Kookie left the series temporarily, but soon came back as a partner in the detective agency. "77 Sunset Strip" forever glamorized a part of Hollywood that has always been in need of some favorable PR.

Zimbalist as Bailey.

Bones, Kirk, and Spock.

STAR TREK®

NBC, 1966-69 (78 episodes)

Theme song: "Theme from Star Trek®" by Gene Roddenberry and Alexander Courage

Major cast members: William Shatner, Leonard Nimoy, DeForest Kelley, James Doohan, Nichelle Nichols, George Takei, Majel Barrett, Walter Koenig (1967-69)

"Space, the final frontier. These are the voyages of the star ship Enterprise. Its five-year mission is to seek out new life and new civilization, and boldly go where no man has gone before." And with those opening words, narrated by Captain James T. Kirk (William Shatner), the crew of the Enterprise was off on its weekly adventure. However, the five-year mission of the Enterprise was cut short — three years short to be exact — due to low Nielsen ratings. In fact, "Star Trek" could be called the most successful failure in television history. The show never ranked higher than 52 in its initial run. The multi-cultural crew of the Enterprise was led by the heroic Captain Kirk. Other regulars included the pointed-eared emotionless Vulcan Spock (Leonard Nimoy), the "simple country doctor" Leonard McCoy (DeForest Kelley) and the spastic chief engineer Montgomery "Scotty" Scott (James Doohan). The brainchild of Gene Roddenberry, the show intergalactic highlights included TV's first interracial kiss between Kirk and communications officer Uhura (Nichelle Nichols), and ongoing battles with the Federation's arch enemies the Klingons and the Romulans. Years after cancellation, the show lived on in reruns and "Star Trek" conventions where fanatics called "Trekkies" or "Trekkers" dressed as assorted aliens, swapped merchandise and paid to see original cast members regale them with anecdotes from their favorite episodes. In 1979, the original crew reunited for the first big screen film, followed up by several sequels. In addition, the show has spawned more television series spin-offs for first run syndication. "Star Trek," as Spock would say, has "lived long and prospered."

THE TWILIGHT ZONE

CBS, 1959-1964 (134 30-minute episodes, 17 one-hour shows)

Theme Song: "Twilight Zone" by Maurius Constant

Major cast members: Hosted by Rod Serling, the show featured an ensemble cast that changed weekly, but included such notable names as Burgess Meredith, Robert Redford, David Wayne, William Shatner, Roddy McDowall, Inger Stevens, Cliff Robertson

Playwright Rod Serling had already written the classic TV drama "Requiem for a Heavyweight" when he decided to turn his focus to science fiction. Serling opened each episode with the familiar theme music in the background and the deadpan words, "There is a fifth dimension as vast as space and as timeless as infinity. It is the middle ground between light and shadow, between science and superstition, and it lies between the pit of man's fears and the summit of his knowledge. This is the dimension of imagination. It is an area we call 'The Twilight Zone.' " Serling, the main creative force behind the series, wrote 89 of the 151 shows. The stories were unusual, offbeat and sometimes concluded with an unexpected ending. Favorite episodes include: "The Dummy" (Cliff Robertson), "The Hitchhiker" (Inger Stevens), "Nightmare at 20,000 Feet" (William Shatner) and "Time Enough to Last" (Burgess Meredith). After three season in a half-hour format, the show expanded to a full hour. However, only 17 one hour shows were shot before returning to the 30-minute format. The show also spawned a 1983 theatrical version that is best remembered as the film that during shooting killed actor Vic Morrow and two children in a helicopter accident. In 1985, (long after the death of Serling), "The Twilight Zone" returned to television. The new shows, now in color and using more elaborate special effects, were mostly new stories, although some remakes of previous episodes were filmed.

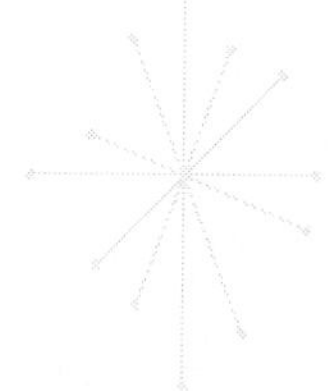

THE UNTOUCHABLES

CBS, 1959-1963 (114 episodes)

Theme Song: "Theme from The Untouchables" by Nelson Riddle

Major cast members: Robert Stack, Jerry Paris (1959-1960), Abel Fernandez, Nick Georgiade, Anthony George (1960), Paul Picerni (1960-63), Steve London (1960-63), Bruch Jordan, Walter Winchell (narrator)

Robert Stack has made a life of crime really pay off. He has "walked the beat" in five television series that have dealt, in one way or another, with the criminal element. Starting in 1959 with his Emmy Award-winning role as Eliot Ness in the Prohibition-era series "The Untouchables," Stack went on to portray the editor of *Crime* magazine in "The Name of the Game," followed by roles on the police-action shows "Most Wanted" and "Strike Force." He most recently served as host of "Unsolved Mysteries," a viewer call-in show that fingers real-life fugitives from justice. However, it is as Eliot Ness that he will best be remembered. The show, based on the life of real treasury department gangbusters, gave audiences the first big dose of television violence. Stack said he based his character on the fact that Ness was brave and "put his money where his mouth was." In fact, his inspiration for the character was Audie Murphy, the most decorated American soldier of World War II. His portrayal of the crusty, no-nonsense agent who nailed Al Capone even won the seal of approval from Ness' widow. In a letter to Stack, she wrote: "I was afraid of a television series about my husband. I loved him very much and am very protective of him. But I'm happy to say the show is decent and good. In particular, I was worried about your interpretation of my husband. I don't know how you did it, maybe by osmosis, but you have picked up several of his characteristics that are quite striking. You are very much like him in attitude." In 1987, Kevin Costner played Eliot Ness in a big screen version of the show.

Robert Stack as Eliot Ness.

A break from the trail.

WAGON TRAIN

NBC, 1957-1962, ABC, 1962-65 (440 episodes)

Theme Song: "(Roll Along) Wagon Train" by Jack Brooks and Sammy Fain

Major cast members: Ward Bond (1957-1961), Robert Horton (1957-1962), Terry Wilson, Frank McGrath, Scott Miller (1961-64), John McIntire (1961-65), Michael Burns (1963-65), Robert Fuller (1963-65)

It was a real ratings horse race between the three reining Westerns of this period — "Wagon Train," "Gunsmoke" and "Bonanza." All took turns bouncing each other from the number one slot. Ward Bond, a veteran of some 200 cowboy movies and a close friend of the two Johns — Wayne and Ford, starred in the 1950 movie *The Wagonmaster*. Seven years later he recreated the role of wagonmaster Seth Adams for the small screen. Sort of like a "Love Boat" set on a stagecoach, Adams helped pioneers (a different guest star each week) safely make the rough and tumble trek from St. Joseph, Missouri, to the West. The weekly roster of guest stars usually dictated the plot and made the programs seem almost like a different movie each week, rather than an ongoing series with a recognizable group of cast regulars. What also made the show different from the other Westerns is that it didn't always rely on outlaws, Indians and gunfights for its stories. Bond died in 1961, during which time the show was the second highest rated in the country. So instead of calling it quits, the producers hired a new wagonmaster, Chris Hale (John McIntire). Hale guided "Wagon Train" to the number one spot in 1962. The theme, performed as an instrumental, was co-written by Jack Brooks, who co-wrote the popular "That's Amore" and two-time Oscar-winner Sammy Fain.

THE WILD WILD WEST

CBS, 1965-1970 (104 episodes)

Theme Song: "The Wild Wild West Theme" by Richard Markowitz

Major cast members: Robert Conrad, Ross Martin

James T. West (Robert Conrad) was sort of like the James Bond of the Western genre. Working as a special undercover agent for President Grant in the 1870s, West traveled in a specially equipped railroad car with his partner, Artemus Gordon (Ross Martin). Gordon was a master at both dialects and disguises and his bag of tricks came in handy when the two confronted a variety of undesirable characters. The duo worked to thwart the efforts of an assortment of criminal groups who were hellbent on taking over all or part of the United States. Most memorable of these criminals was the evil genius Dr. Miguelito Loveless (played by dwarf Michael Dunn). In an ongoing role, Dr. Loveless was an antagonist in the style of Professor Moriarty from the Sherlock Holmes books. The series was also populated with a bevy of attractive women in need of assistance from the most obliging Mr. West. Some of the special effects and gadgets used were so futuristic you had to suspend disbelief to believe that this show was set in the nineteenth century. Several years later West and Gordon reunited for some "Wild Wild West" TV movies.

Martin and Conrad.

THE WONDERFUL WORLD OF DISNEY

All three major networks, 1954-1990

Theme Song: "When You Wish Upon a Star" by Ned Washington and Leigh Harline

Hosts: Walt Disney (1954-1966), Michael Eisner (1986-1990)

This show had many different names during its 34 season run (it took a two year hiatus in 1984-85) on all three major networks—"Disneyland," "Walt Disney Presents," Walt Disney's Wonderful World of Color," "The Wonderful World of Disney," "The Disney Sunday Movie" and "The Magical World of Disney." It also has the distinction of being the longest-running prime-time series in TV history. Disney, a true visionary, was the first major studio head to take the leap into television. He was enticed by the struggling ABC because the network agreed to invest in an elaborate amusement park called Disneyland. The move paid off for both parties. "Disneyland" became a tourist sensation and the show became ABC's first major hit series. In the early years the program was structured like a theme park with such segments as "Adventureland," ("Sammy, the Way Out Seal"); "Fantasyland," ("The Legend of Sleepy Hollow"); "Tomorrowland," (this could include a documentary on space travel); and "Frontierland," featuring "Davy Crockett." The adventures of this real-life Western action hero became a major component of the show and made a star out of Fess Parker and a hit record from its theme, "The Ballad of Davy Crockett." It was hard to find a kid in the mid '50s who wasn't wearing a coon-skin hat. There were other presentations beyond the four segments, including animated cartoons featuring Mickey Mouse, full-length films such as "Babes in Toyland" starring Ray Bolger, Tommy Sands and Annette Funicello and documentaries covering a variety of topics. The show's theme, "When You Wish Upon a Star" was an Oscar-winner written for the 1940 film *Pinocchio.*

THE
THEME
SONGS

THE ADDAMS FAMILY

Theme Song: The Addams Family Theme

Music and Lyrics by
VIC MIZZY

F7
B♭
Cm7
3fr
F7
B♭
no chord
peo - ple come to see 'em, they real - ly are a scree-um, the Add-ams Fam - i - ly.
(Spoken:) Neat.
Sweet.
B♭
Cm7
3fr
F7
B♭
Petite. (Sung:) So get a witch-es shawl on, a broom-stick you can crawl on, we're
Cm7
3fr
F7
B♭
gon - na pay a call on the Add - ams Fam - i - ly.

THE ADVENTURES OF SUPERMAN

Theme Song: Superman

Words and Music by
LEON KLATZKIN

A
E
A
E
E7
3
A
E/G#
A
B7/F#
E
E7
A
3
D
Bm7
2fr
A/E
E7
A
F
3
Ab
4fr
F
3
B/F#
F#
B/F#
F#
F#7
B

ALFRED HITCHCOCK PRESENTS

Theme Song: Funeral March of a Marionette

By CHARLES GOUNOD

Mysteriously

AMERICAN BANDSTAND

Theme Song: Bandstand Boogie

Words by BARRY MANILOW
and BRUCE SUSSMAN
Music by CHARLES ALBERTINE

B7 B♭maj7
1 A
mu - sic they play on the Band - stand.
dad are so proud, I'm on Band - stand.
(Band - stand.) We're go - in'
2 A
A A/C♯ D Cdim/E♭
(Band stand.) And I'll jump and, hey, I may ev - en show 'em my
all you Joe's here goes my A - mer - i - can
A/E B7/D♯ D9 C♯7+5 C13
hand - stand,
hand - stand;
be - cause I'm on, be - cause I'm on
be - cause I'm on, be - cause I'm on
B7 B♭maj7 A G♯ A A/C♯
the A - mer - i - can Band - stand.
the A - mer - i - can Band - stand.
When we dance real slow I'll show
As we dance real slow I'm show-

D
Cdim/E♭
A/E
B7/D♯
A
D9
C♯7+5
C13
all the guys in the grand - stand,
in' the guys in the grand - stand,
what a swing - er I am; I am
that I like my girl, but I
B7
B♭maj7
To Coda
A
A6
on A - mer - i - can Band - stand.
love A - mer - i - can
We're go - in' hop - pin', we're go - in'
D9
hop - pin' to - day where things are pop - pin' the Phil - a - del - phi - a way. We're gon - na
D/E
B7
B♭maj7
drop in on all the mus - ic they play on the Band - stand. Band - stand.

Bm/A
B/A
Band - stand.
Band - stand.
Band - stand.
What - da - ya know, here on the show read - y to go,
Bm7/E
A6
what a pro! Hey! I'm mak - in' my mark; Gee, this
D9
C#7+5
C13
B7
Bbmaj7
joint is jump - in'. They made such a fuss just to see us ar - rive.

A
D7/A
A6
Hey! It's Mis - ter Dick Clark; what a place you've got here,
D9
B7
B♭maj7
swell spot, the mu - sic's hot here. Best in the East, give it
A
D.S. al Coda
at least a sev - en - ty - five! Now for
CODA
A
Band - stand.

A6
Dm6/B
A6
The sing - er's
Bb6
Eb9
croon - in', he ain't the great - est, but gee, my ba - by's swoon - in', in front of
hop - pin', and we'll be hop - pin' all day where things are pop - pin' the Phil - a -
Eb/F
all of T. V. So if you tune in, you'll see my ba - by and me on the
del - phi - a way. And you can drop in on all the mu - sic they play on the
C
Bmaj7
1
2
Guitar Tacet
Band - stand, Band - stand. And now we're Band - stand. And we'll rock and roll and
Band - stand,

Stroll on A - mer - i - can, Lin - dy Hop and Slop, it's A mer - i - can
Eb9
D7+5
Db13
C7
Bmaj7
tune in, I'm on, turn on, I'm in, I'm on!
Bb6
Eb9
Eb/F
To - day,
C7
Bmaj7
Bb6
Band - stand.

BEN CASEY

Theme Song: Theme from "Ben Casey"

By DAVID RAKSIN

To Coda
(Optional in R.H.)
mf

D.S. al Coda
f
sfz
sfz
CODA
ff
fff

BONANZA

Theme Song: Bonanza

Words and Music by JAY LIVINGSTON and RAY EVANS

C
We're not a one to sad - dle up and run, bo - nan - za!
G7sus
G7
An - y - one of us who starts a lit - tle fuss
Dm7/G
G7
C
knows he can count on me!
G
C
G/D
A9
One for four four for one, this we guar - an -

D9
G
tee! We got a right to pick a lit - tle fight, bo -
D7sus
nan - za! If an - y - one fights
D7
Am7/D
D7
1 G
an - y - one of us, he's got - ta fight with me!
f
2 G
me!
f

THE BEVERLY HILLBILLIES

Theme Song: The Ballad of Jed Clampett

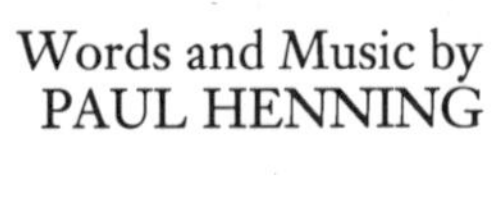

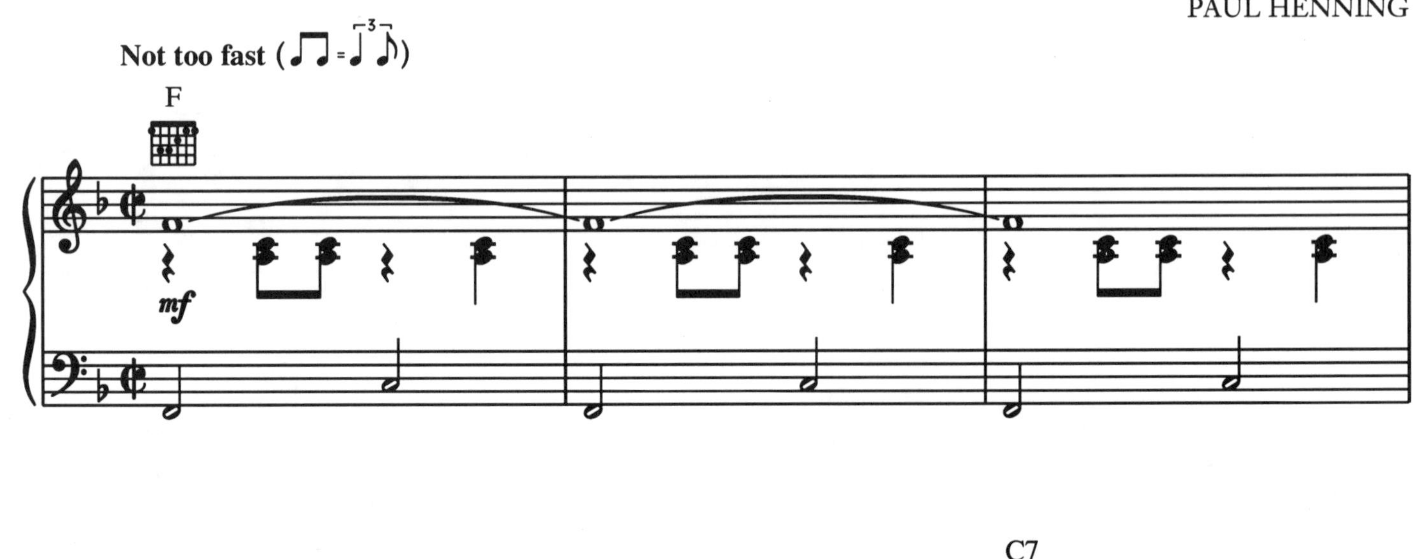

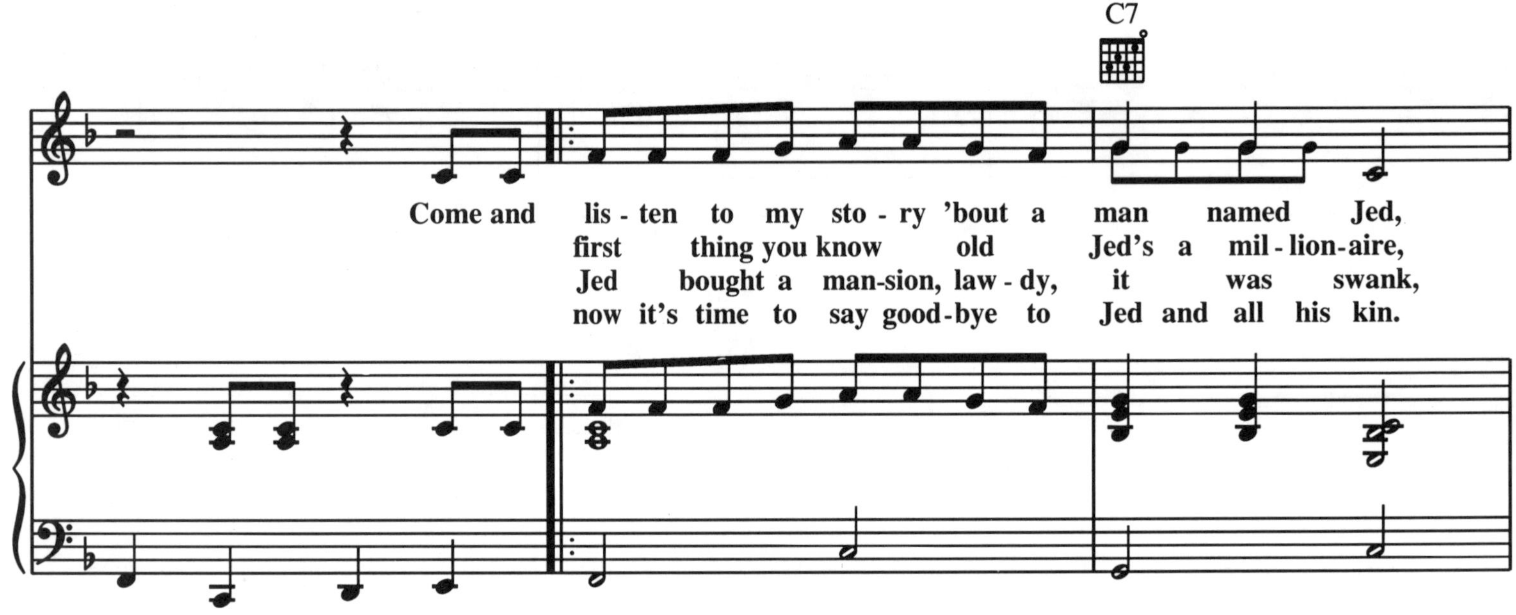

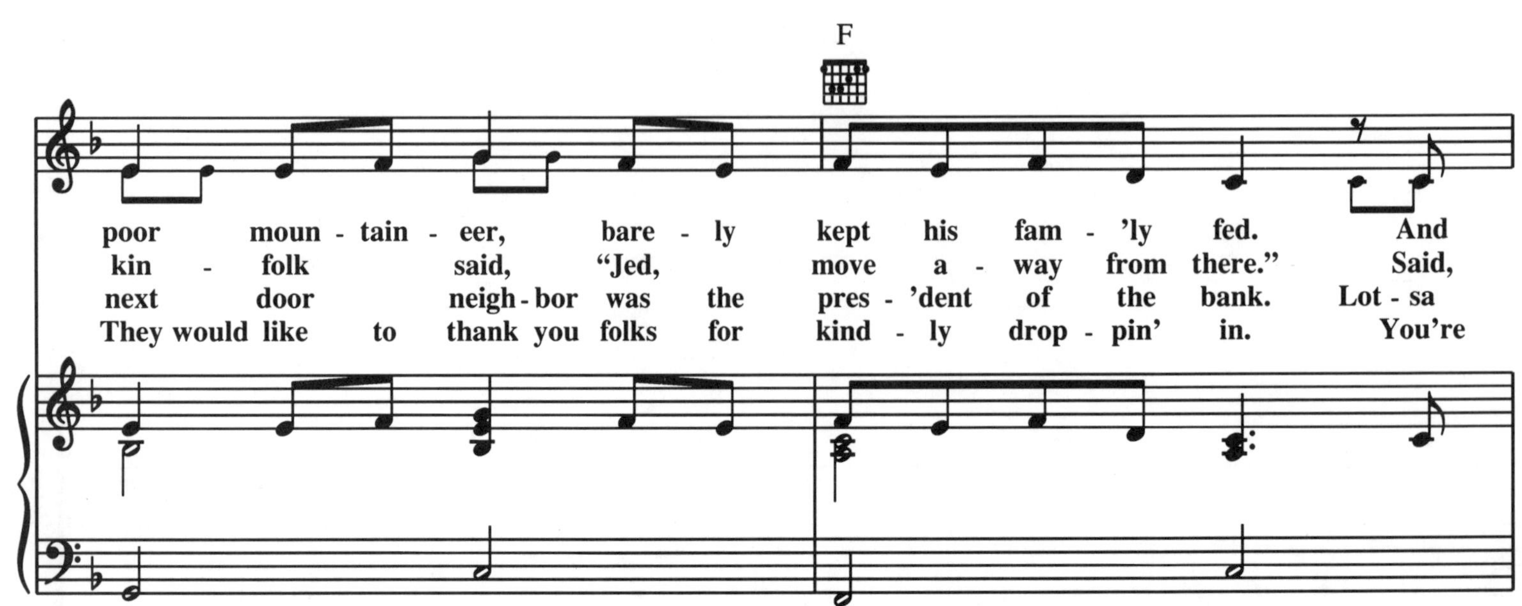

F7
B♭
Bdim7
then one day, he was shoot - in' at some food, and
"Cal - i - for - ny is the place you ought - a be." So they
folks ob - ject - ed, but the bank - er found no fault, 'cause
all in - vit - ed back a - gain to this lo - cal - i - ty to
C7
F
up through the ground came a - bub - bl - in' crude.
load - ed up the truck and they moved to Bev - er - ly.
old Jed's mil - lions was a - lay - in' in the vault.
have a heap - in' help - in' of their hos - pi - tal - i - ty.
Oil, that is! Black gold, Texas Tea!
Hills, that is! Swimmin' pools, movie stars!
Cash, that is! Capital gains, depletion money!
Hillbilly, that is! Set a spell, take your shoes off!
1–3
4
C7
F
Well, the
Old
Well,
Y'all come back, ya hear?

BEWITCHED

Theme Song: Theme from "Bewitched"

Words and Music by JACK KELLER
and HOWARD GREENFIELD

Fm6
Em7
E7♭9
Am
you were do - ing, I looked in your eyes. That
Am7
D9
4fr
G7sus
brand of woo that you've been brew - in' took me by sur - prise.
G7
C♯dim7
Dm7
G7
You witch, you witch,
Dm7
G7
E♭dim7
Em7
one thing is for sure that stuff you pitch

A7
Em7
just has - n't got a cure.
A7
Fmaj7
My heart was un - der
F♯dim7
C/G
B♭
A7
lock and key but some - how it got un - hitched.
3
Dm7
A7♭9
6fr
Dm7
I nev - er thought my heart

Dm7
E♭dim7
Em7
B7♭9
E7♭9
could be had
but now I'm caught and I'm
Am
Dm7
Dm7/G
kind-a glad to be
be-
1
C6
A♭13
3fr
G13
2fr
C♯dim7
Dm7
witched.
Be - witched
2
C6
G7♯5
C6
witched.

THE BRADY BUNCH

Theme Song: The Brady Bunch

Words and Music by SHERWOOD SCHWARTZ
and FRANK DEVOL

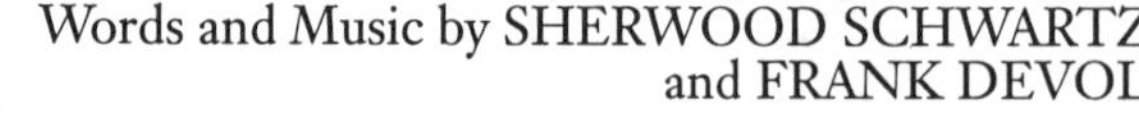

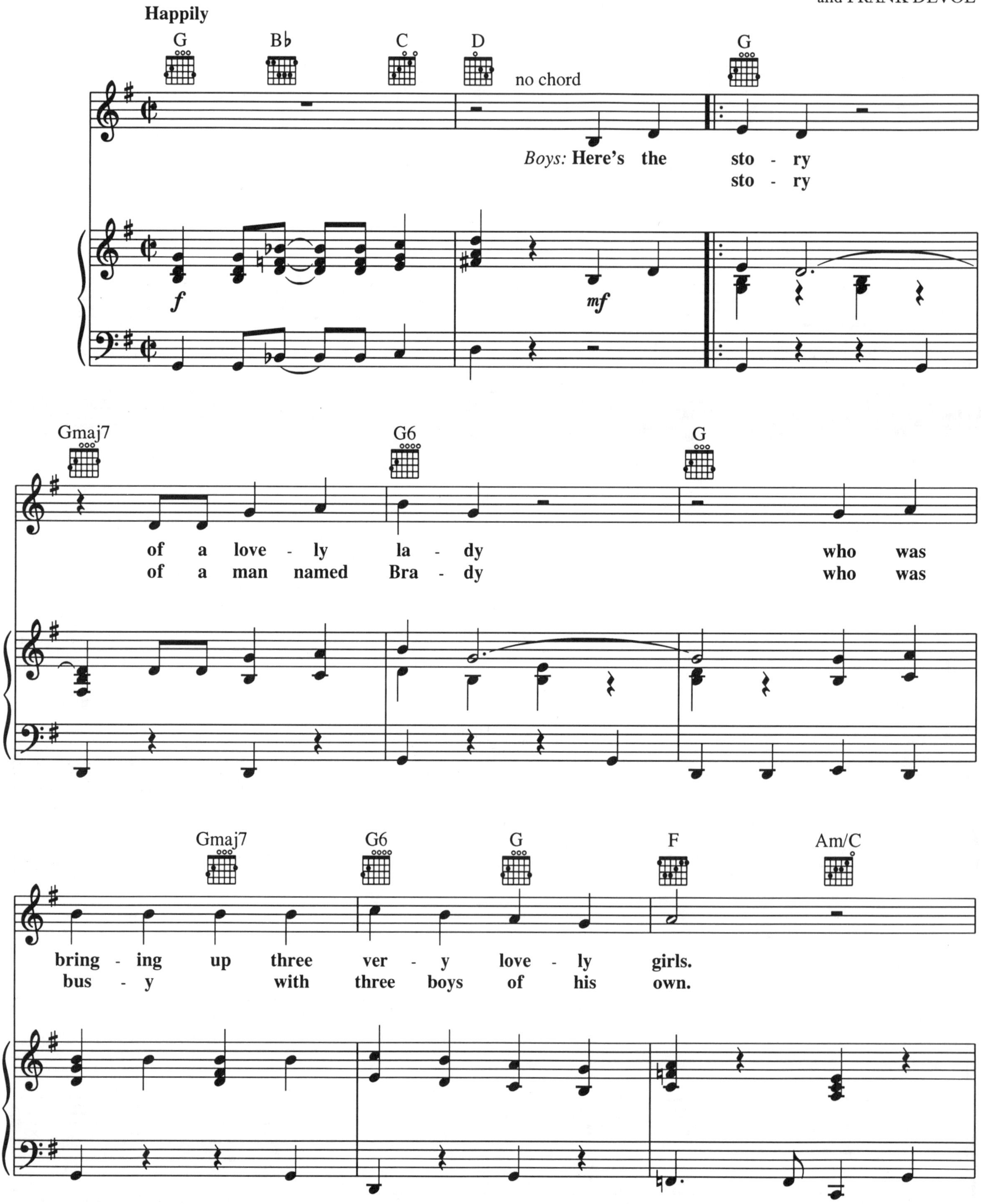
Happily
G Bb C D no chord G
Boys: Here's the sto - ry
sto - ry
Gmaj7 G6 G
of a love - ly la - dy who was
of a man named Bra - dy who was
Gmaj7 G6 G F Am/C
bring - ing up three ver - y love - ly girls.
bus - y with three boys of his own.

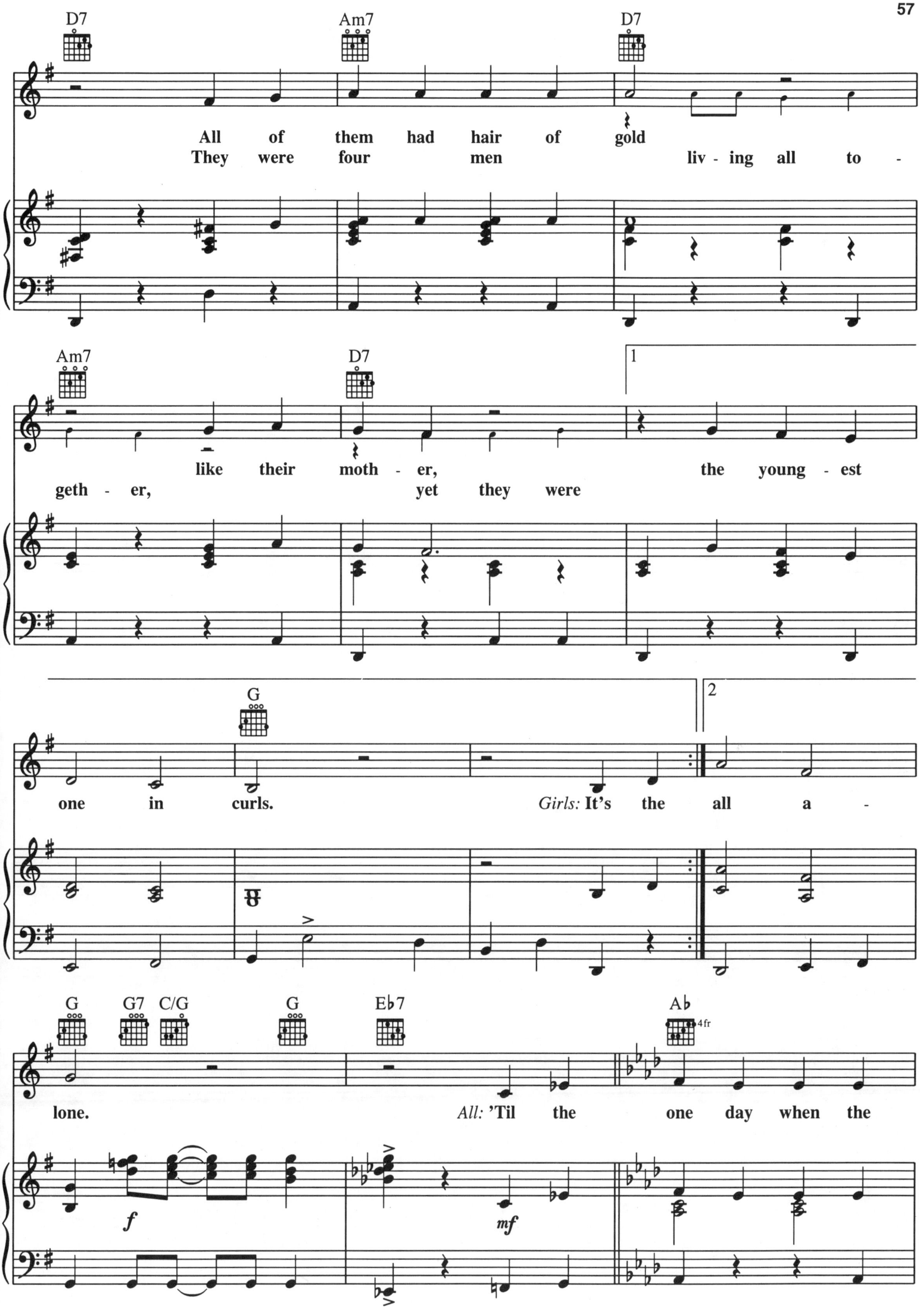
D7
Am7
D7
All of them had hair of gold
They were four men liv - ing all to -
Am7
D7
1
like their moth - er, the young - est
geth - er, yet they were
G
2
one in curls. Girls: It's the all a -
G
G7
C/G
G
E♭7
A♭
4fr
lone. All: 'Til the one day when the
f
mf

A♭maj7
A♭6
3fr
A♭
4fr
la - dy met this fel - low, and they
B♭m7
knew that it was much more than a hunch
E♭
3fr
B♭m7
E♭7
that this group must some - how form a
B♭m7
E♭7
B♭m7
fam - 'ly. That's the way we all be -

Eb7
Ab
4fr
came the Bra - dy Bunch. The Bra - dy
Db
Db7
4fr
Gb/Db
Db
Ab
4fr
Ab7
4fr
Db/Ab
4fr
Ab
4fr
Bunch, the Bra - dy Bunch. That's the
Bb
Eb
3fr
Eb7
way we be - came the Bra - dy
Ab
4fr
Db/Ab
4fr
Ab
4fr
no chord
Ab
4fr
Ab7
4fr
Db/Ab
4fr
Ab
4fr
Bunch.
f

THE COURTSHIP OF EDDIE'S FATHER

Theme Song: Courtship of Eddie's Father

Words and Music by
HARRY NILSSON

B
People, let me tell you about him; he's so much fun, whether we're
talk - in' man to man or wheth - er we're talk - in' son to son 'cause he's my
best friend.
Yeah, he's my best friend.
A
D/E
A
Repeat and Fade
La la la la la la la la la la la la

THE CAROL BURNETT SHOW

Theme Song: I'm So Glad We Had This Time Together

By JOE HAMILTON

Slowly

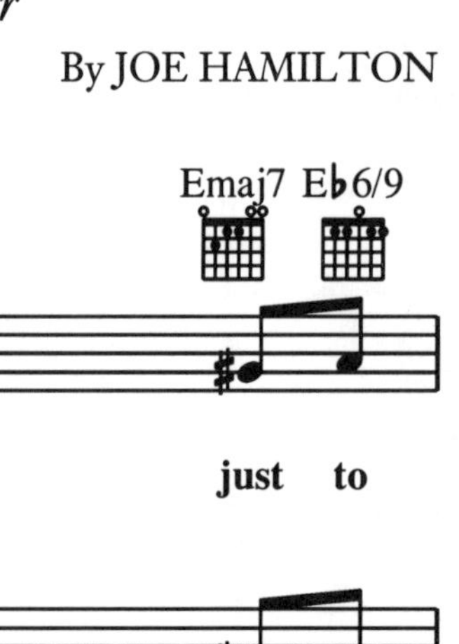

Emaj7 E♭6/9 Dm7 A♭9♭5 G9sus Cmaj7 Emaj7 E♭6/9

I'm so glad we had this time to - geth - er, just to

Dm7 A♭9♭5 G9sus Cmaj7 Dm7 G7

have a laugh or sing a song. Seems we just get start - ed and be - fore you

Em11 A7♯5(♭9) Emaj7 E♭6/9 Dm7 A♭9♭5 G9sus C6 A7♭9 Emaj7 E♭6/9

know it, comes the time we have to say so long. There's a

Dm7 A♭9♭5 G9sus Cmaj7 Emaj7 E♭6/9 Dm7 A♭9♭5 G9sus
time you put a - side for dream-in', and a time for things you have to do.
Cmaj7 Dm7 G7 Em9 A7♯5(♭9)
But the time I like the best is an - y eve - ning I can
Dm7 G13 C6 Bm7 E7
spend a mo-ment here with you. When the time comes and I'm feel - ing
Amaj7 F♯m7 F7 Bm7/E E9 Amaj7 F♯m7 C♯m7 F♯7
lone - ly, when I'm feel - in' oh so blue, I just sit back and think of you

Bmaj7
G#m7
C#m11
F#9
F#m7
F7
Emaj7
Eb6/9
on - ly and the hap - pi - ness still comes_ through. I'm so
Dm7
Ab7b5
G9sus
Cmaj7
Emaj7
Eb6/9
Dm7
Ab7b5
G9sus
glad we had this time to - geth - er 'cause it makes me feel that I be - long.
Cmaj7
Dm7
G7
Em11
A7#5(b9)
Seems we just get start - ed and be-fore you know it, guess it's
Dm7
G13
C6
F9
C6/E
Ebdim7
Dm7
Dbmaj7
Cmaj9
time for me to say, "So long."

GET SMART

Theme Song: Get Smart

By IRVING SZATHMARY

Fm
D♭7
C7
Fm
D♭7
C7
Fm
D♭7
C7
Fm
D♭7
C7
C+
B+
B♭+
D♭7
Fm
D♭7
C7♭9
Fm
B♭m6

Gbm6
Bbm6
C7b9
Fm
Db7
C7
Fm
Db7
C7
Fm
Db7
C7
Fm
Db7
C7
C+
B+
Bb+
Db7
Fm
C7
Fm

MAKE ROOM FOR DADDY/ THE DANNY THOMAS SHOW

Theme Song: Danny Boy (Londonderry Air)

Words by FREDERICK EDWARD WEATHERLY
Music is Irish Traditional

C/G
G7
C
G7
you must go and I must bide. But come ye
C
F/C
G7/C
C
G7
back when sum - mer's in the mead - ow, or when the
C/E
F
C
Gsus
G
G7
val - ley's hush'd and white with snow. And I'll be
C
C7
F
C
Am
F
D7/A
there in sun - shine or in shad - ow, oh, Dan - ny

C/G
G7
C
C7
F
boy, oh, Dan - ny boy, I love you so!
C
Am
G7
C
C7
F
Em/D
But when ye come, and all the flowr's are dy - ing, if I am
C/E
F
C/G
Am
F
G7
C
C7
dead, as dead I well may be, ye'll come and find the place where I am
F
Dm
A♭6
C
Dm
G7
ly - ing, and kneel and say an A - ve there for

C G7/C Am/C Cmaj7 F/C G7/C C F C E7/B
me. And I shall hear, though soft you tread a - bove me, and all my
Am F Em Gsus G G7 C F
grave will warm-er, sweet-er be. For you will bend and tell me that you
C Am C7#5/E F Ab6 C F/G G7 1 C
love me, and I shall sleep in peace un - til you come to me!
2 C
me!

THE DONNA REED SHOW

Theme Song: The Donna Reed Theme

By JACK KELLER
and HOWARD GREENFIELD

D
Bm
Em7
A7
D(add9)
2fr
Bm
Em7
A7
D
Bm
Em7
A7
F♯m7♭5
4fr
B7
Em
Em7♭5
F♯m7
Bm7
2fr
E13
Em7
A7
D6

FATHER KNOWS BEST

Theme Song: Father Knows Best Theme

By DON FERRIS
and IRVING FRIEDMAN

3
1
2

THE FLINTSTONES

Theme Song: (Meet) The Flintstones

Gm7
C7
2
Fmaj7
B♭7
A7
ry.
Let's ride
E♭7♭9
D7
A♭13♭5
with the fam - 'ly down the street,
G7
D♭7♭9
C7
through the cour - te - sy of Fred's two
G♭13♭5
Fmaj7
Gm7
Am7
feet. When you're with the Flint - stones,

B♭maj7
Fmaj7
Gm7
C7
Have a ya ba da ba gay old
F
Fmaj7
Gm7
time. When you're with the
Am7
B♭maj7
E♭maj7
Fmaj7
A♭13
Flint - stones, have a ya ba da ba
Gm7
G♭13♭9
Fmaj7
A♭13
Gm7
G♭13♭9
doo time, a ya ba doo time,

Half time
Fmaj7
Ab13
Gm7
C7b9
Fmaj7
you'll have a gay old time.
Swing
Gm7
Am7
We'll see Barn - ey, we'll see Bet - ty, Bam - bam, Peb - bles,
Bbmaj7
Fmaj7
Ab13
Gm7
C7b9
Di - no, too. You'll have a gay old
F6/9
E7#9
F6/9
E7#9
Fmaj7
time.

HAZEL

Theme Song: Hazel

Words and Music by HOWARD GREENFIELD
and JACK KELLER

B♭/F
D7/F♯
Gm
3fr
C7
Cas - sa - no - va. It's your per - son -
Cm7/F
G♭7
F7
al - i - ty that wins them o - ver.
Cm
3fr
Cm(maj7)
Cm7
3fr
You may nev - er be a mil - lion - aire,
F7
B♭
B♭maj7
Haz - el. Count your friends and you don't have to

Dm7♭5
G7
Cm9
care,
Haz - el.
You've got more than
E♭m6
B♭
C7
wealth un - told; you've got a heart of sol - id gold. We
F9
Cm7
3 fr
F9
F7♭9
1 B♭
love you, Haz - el, just be - cause you're you.
2 B♭
A♭6
3 fr
B♭6

HOGAN'S HEROES

Theme Song: Hogan's Heroes March

By JERRY FIELDING

F C7 1 F C7sus C7 2 F C7sus C7
that's what we're he - roes for. for.
F C7
What's a he - ro do? Well, we're not gon - na tell ya cos
F F7 B♭ Gm
we wish we knew. That's why we he - roes are so few. We've got a
F Dm Gm B♭ F C
slo - gan from Colo - nel Ho - gan and Colo - nel Ho - gan's a he - ro

F
D
G
D7
too.
Nev - er flinch, boys, nev - er be a - fraid,
3
G
he - roes are not born, boys, he - roes all are made.
G7
C
Am
G
Em
Ask not why, boys, nev - er say die, boys, an - swer the call, re -
Am
D
G
D7
G
mem - ber we'll all be he - roes for - ev - er - more.

HOWDY DOODY

Theme Song: It's Howdy Doody Time

Words and Music by
EDWARD GEORGE KEAN

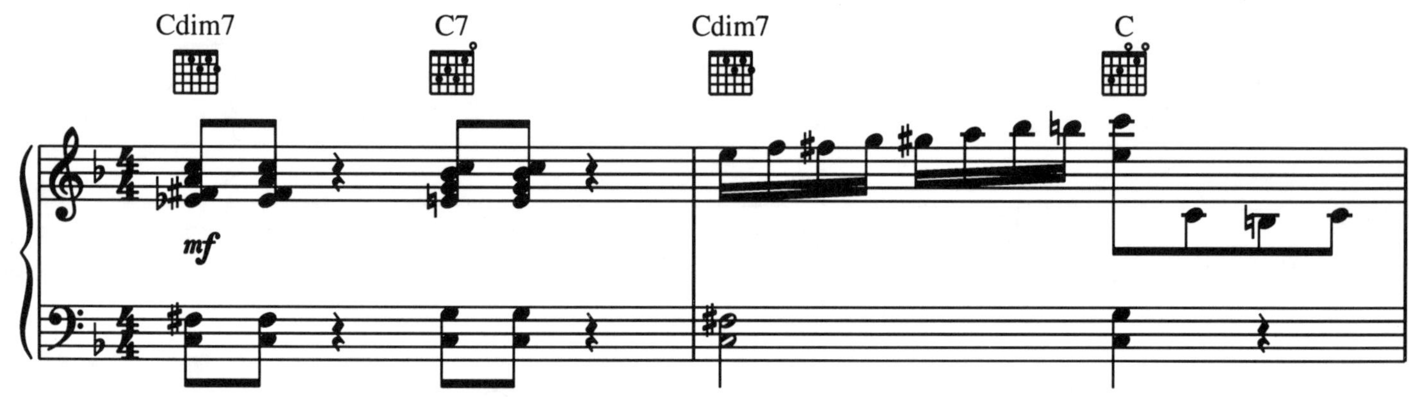

C
Doo - dy time, it's How - dy Doo - dy time. Bob Smith and
G7
C
How - dy Doo say how - dy doo to you. Let's give a
rous - ing cheer 'cause How - dy Doo - dy's here. It's time to
G7
C6
start the show, so, kids, let's go!

I DREAM OF JEANNIE

Theme Song: Jeannie

By HUGH MONTENEGRO
and BUDDY KAYE

G9
G+
3 fr
C
C♯dim7
- to! The rain goes. She blinks. Up comes the rain - bows!
Dm
Dm7
G9
G+
3 fr
C
Cars stop, e - ven the train goes slow when
C7
Fm7
B♭7
she goes by! She paints sun - shine on ev - 'ry
E♭maj7
3 fr
Cm7
3 fr
Fm
raf - ter, sprin - kles the air with laugh - ter. We're close

Dm7♭5
G7sus
G7
no chord
as a quar - ter af - ter three. There's no one like
Dm
Dm7
G7
G+
3fr
C
Jean - nie. I'll in - tro - duce her to you, but
C♯dim7
Dm
Dm7
G7
G+
3fr
it's no use, sir, 'cause my Jean - nie's in love with
1
C
me!
2
C
Gm7/D
3fr
D♭7♭5
C
me!

I LOVE LUCY

Theme Song: I Love Lucy

Lyric by HAROLD ADAMSON
Music by ELIOT DANIEL

Amaj7
Dm7
A♭7♯5
G13
how we love mak - ing up a - gain.
Cmaj7
Lu - cy kiss - es like
Dm7
G7♭9
Cmaj7
no one can.
She's my mis - sus and
Cmaj7/D
C+/D
D♯dim7
Em7
I'm her man;
And life is heav -

C
Am7
D7
D♯dim7
- en you see 'cause
C
Dm7
G7
C
Em7
I love Lu - cy, yes, I love Lu -
A9
D9
Dm7/G
G7
- cy and Lu - cy loves
1 C
A♭7
G7
2 C
Dm7/G
C6
me. me.

THE JACK BENNY SHOW

Theme Song: Love in Bloom

Words and Music by LEO ROBIN
and RALPH RAINGER

G
Am7/D
D7
Gmaj7/D
G6/D
3fr
Am I on earth?
Am7/D
D7
Am7/D
D7
G
Am I in Heav'n? Can it be the trees that
B7
Em
C
Am
3
fill the breeze with rare and mag - ic per - fume? Oh
D7
D7♯5
D7♯5/G
5fr
G
no, it is - n't the trees, it's love in bloom!

Am7/D D7 G B7 Em
Can it be the spring that seems to bring the
C Am D7
stars right in - to my room? Oh no, it is - n't the
D7/G G
spring, it's love in bloom.
Bm F#7 Bm F#7
My heart was a des - ert, you plant-ed a seed,

Bm
F#7
Bm
Am6
5fr
Am/D
D7
and this is the flow - er; this hour of sweet ful - fill - ment!
G
B7
Em
C
It is all a dream, the joy su-preme that came to us in the
Bbdim7
G6/B
Bbdim7
Am7/D
D7
gloom? You know it is - n't a dream, it's
1
D7/G
G
Ddim7
D7
love in bloom.
2
D7/G
G
Gdim7
G
love in bloom.

THE JETSONS

Theme Song: Jetsons Main Theme

Words and Music by WILLIAM HANNA,
JOSEPH BARBERA and HOYT CURTIN

D♭7
G♭
Jane, his wife.
G♭dim
G♭
D7
G
Daugh - ter Ju - dy
Gdim
G
3

D7
G
Eb7
Ab
Abdim
Ab
His boy El - roy
Eb7
Ab
Eb
(Spoken:) And
Ab/Eb
Eb7
Ab
Ro - sy the ro - bot maid.
Abdim
Ab
A/C#
A7b5
Ab

LASSIE

Theme Song: The Secret of Silent Hills

By WILLIAM LAVA
and CHARLES NEWMAN

Ebmaj7
3fr
Ab/Eb
Bb7
Eb
3fr
In the hush, I heard the whip - poor -
Bb7
Eb7
Ab
4fr
Fm6/Ab
6fr
Cm
3fr
wills re - veal the se - cret of the
Fm7
Bb7
Eb
3fr
Ab
4fr
Bb7
si - lent hills. Not a
Eb
3fr
Ab
4fr
Bb7
Eb
3fr
se - cret men scheme and plot for,

G7sus
G7
Cm
3fr
Cm7/F
F7
on - ly true words we should not for -
Fm7/B♭
B♭7
E♭maj7
3fr
A♭/E♭
B♭7
get. Love can cure the
E♭
3fr
B♭7
E♭7
A♭
4fr
Fm6/A♭
6fr
world of all its ills, and that's the
Cm
3fr
Fm7
B♭7
E♭
3fr
se - cret of the si - lent hills.
rit.

LEAVE IT TO BEAVER

Theme Song: The Toy Parade

By D. KAHN,
M. LENARD and M. GREENE

Gm C F Gm
ging - ham cat in a sol - dier's hat is wav - ing a chi - nese
C F Gm C
fan, a plas - tic clown in a wed - ding gown is
F C7 F F#7 B7♭5 B♭7 A7
danc - ing with Rag - ge - dy Ann. Fee fie
Dm
fid - dle dee dee they're cross - ing the liv - ing room floor,

G7
C7
fee fie fid - dle dee dee they're up to the din - ing room
F
Gm
C
door. They call a halt for a choc - 'late malt or
F
Gm
Gm7
C9
F
cook - ies and lem - on - ade, then off they go with a
Gm
C
F
C7
A♭6
G7
G♭maj7
F
ho ho ho right back to their toy pa - rade.

THE LIFE AND LEGEND OF WYATT EARP

Theme Song: The Life and Legend of Wyatt Earp

E♭7
West - ern fron - tier. The
peace - a - ble life. Some
dealt him his hand. While
or - der pre - vail. And
A♭
B♭m
A♭
4fr
West, it was law - less, but one man was
goods and some chat - tel, a few head of
out - laws were loot - in' and kill - in' and
none can de - ny it the le - gend of
B♭m
A♭
B♭m
B♭7
flaw - less and his is the sto - ry you'll
cat - tle, a home and a sweet lov - ing
shoot - in', he knew that he must take a
Wy - att for - ev - er will live on the
A♭
A♭
C7
hear.
wife.
stand.
trail.
Wy - att Earp,

Db
Ab
4fr
Fm
Bb7
Wy - att Earp brave, cour - a - geous and
Eb7
Ab
4fr
C7
bold.
Long live his fame and
Db
Ab
4fr
Eb7
long live his glo - ry and long may his sto - ry be
1-3
Ab
4fr
4
Ab
4fr
told.
When
Now
He
told.

THE LONE RANGER

Theme Song: The William Tell Overture

By G. ROSSINI

Bb7
Eb
3fr
Eb+
Ab
4fr
Eb
3fr
Bb7
Eb
3fr
Fm/Ab
F/A
Bb
Bb7
Eb
3fr
Eb+
Ab
4fr
Eb
3fr
N.C.
Bb7
Eb
3fr

MANNIX

Theme Song: Mannix

By LALO SCHIFRIN

Bright Jazz Waltz (♫ = ♩ ♪ triplet)

F7#9(#11) Bb13 Eb7#9(#11) Ab13 Dbmj7#11

f *mf*

C7#9(#11) N.C. F Ab Bb

ff *p* *mf*

F6 Cm7

F6 Cm7 F9sus F7sus

B♭maj7
B♭6
A7♭5
A7
Dm7
G7♭5
G7
C♯m7
F♯♭5
F♯7
Bm7
E7sus
E9
p
f
Amaj7
A
A♯dim7
A♯m7♭5
Bm7
E9
C♯m7
F♯m
Dm7(add4)
Dm7
G7

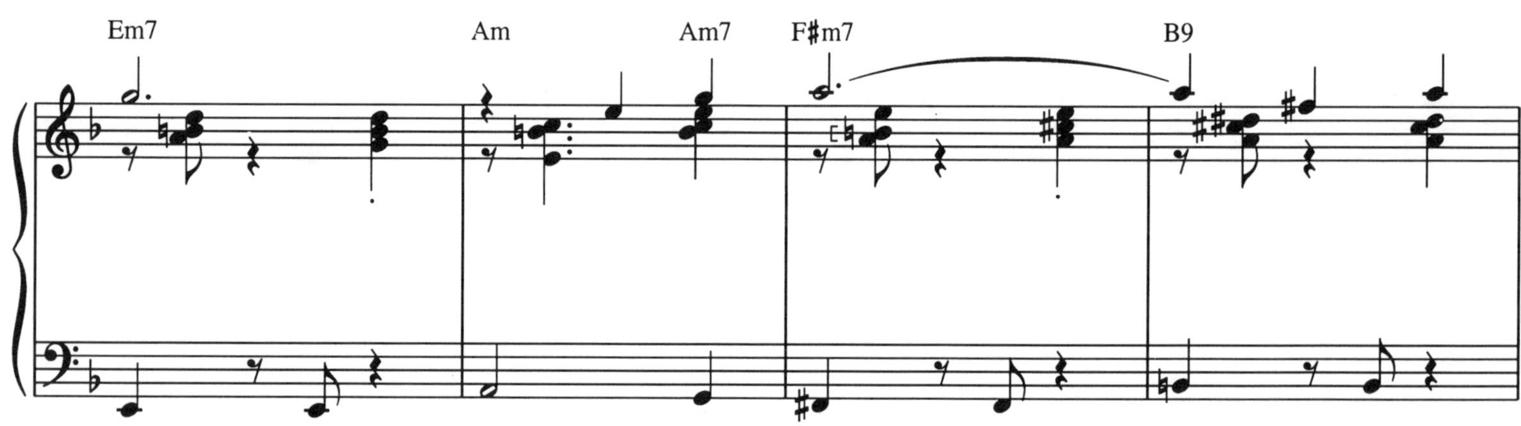
Em7
Am
Am7
F♯m7
B9

Gm
Gm(maj)7
Gm7
C9sus
C7
dim. poco a poco

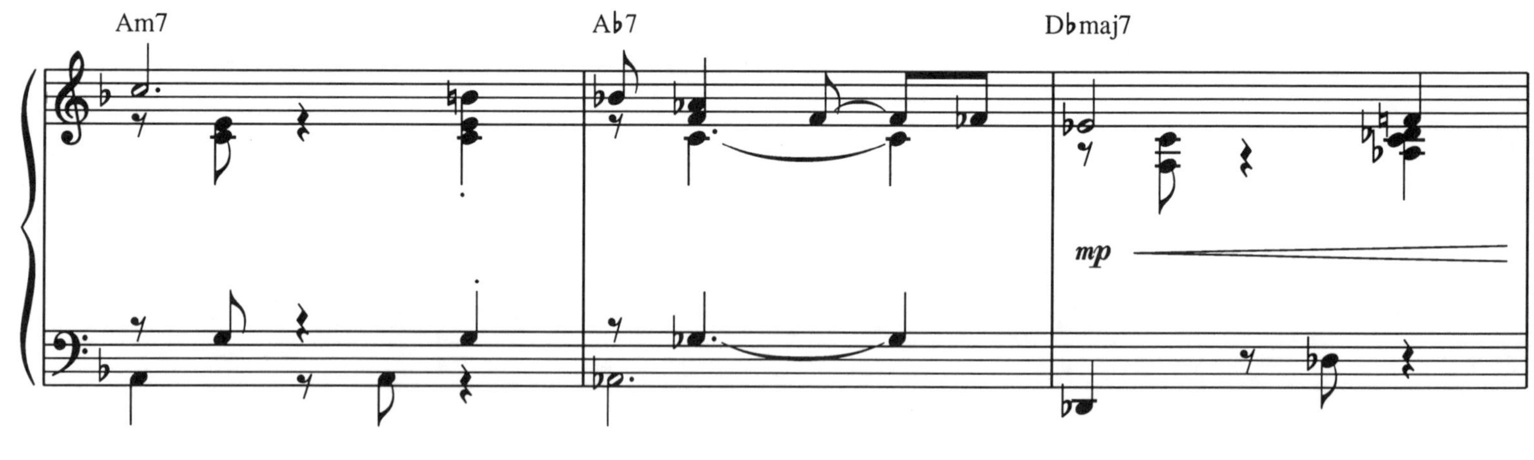
Am7
A♭7
D♭maj7
mp

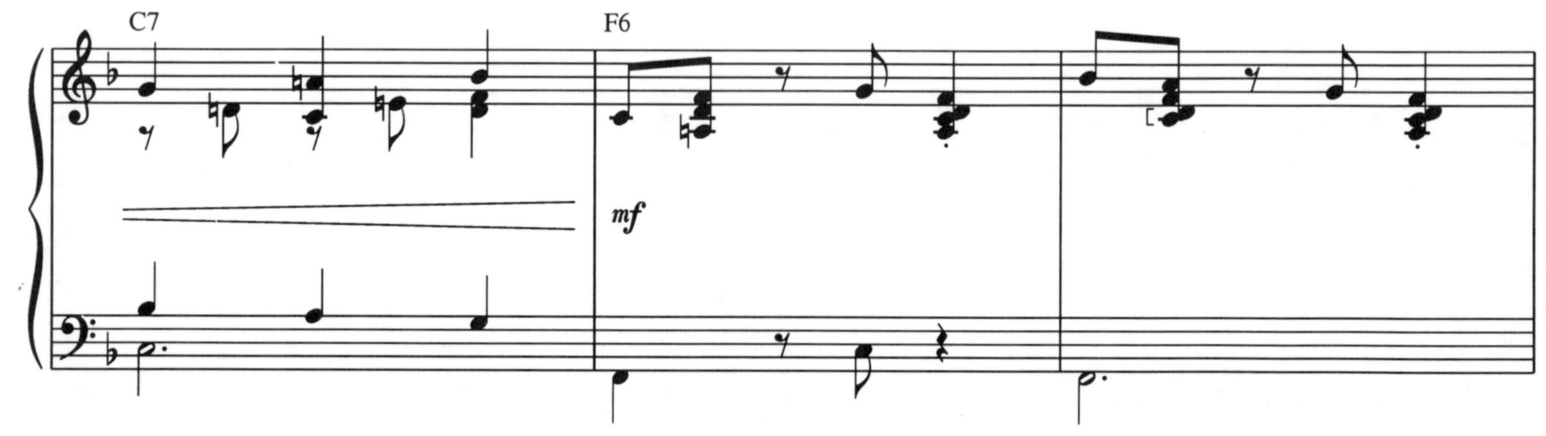
C7
F6
mf

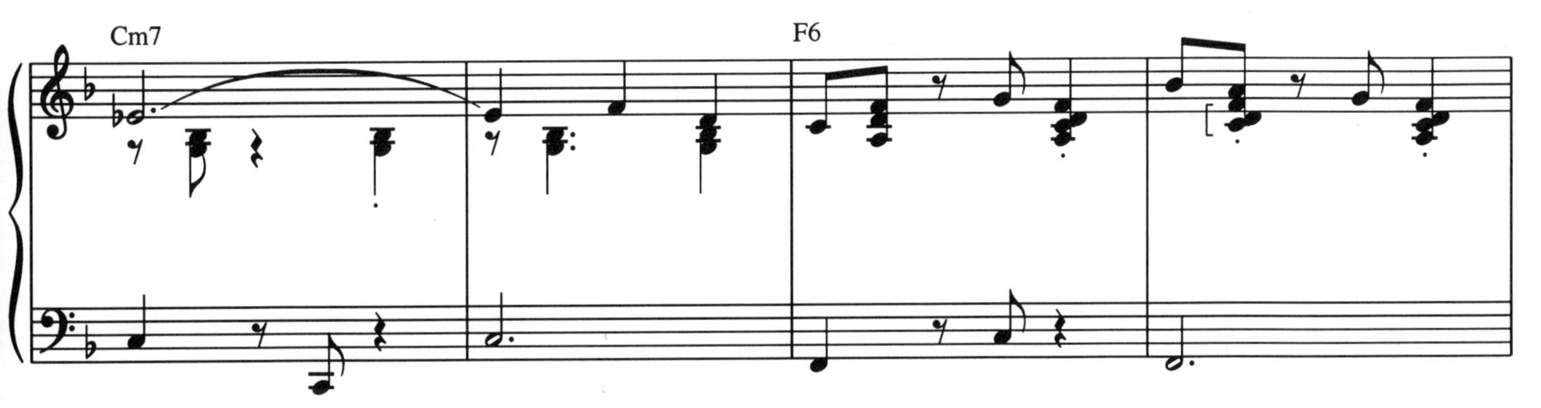
Cm7
F6

Cm7
F9sus
F7sus
B♭maj7
B♭6

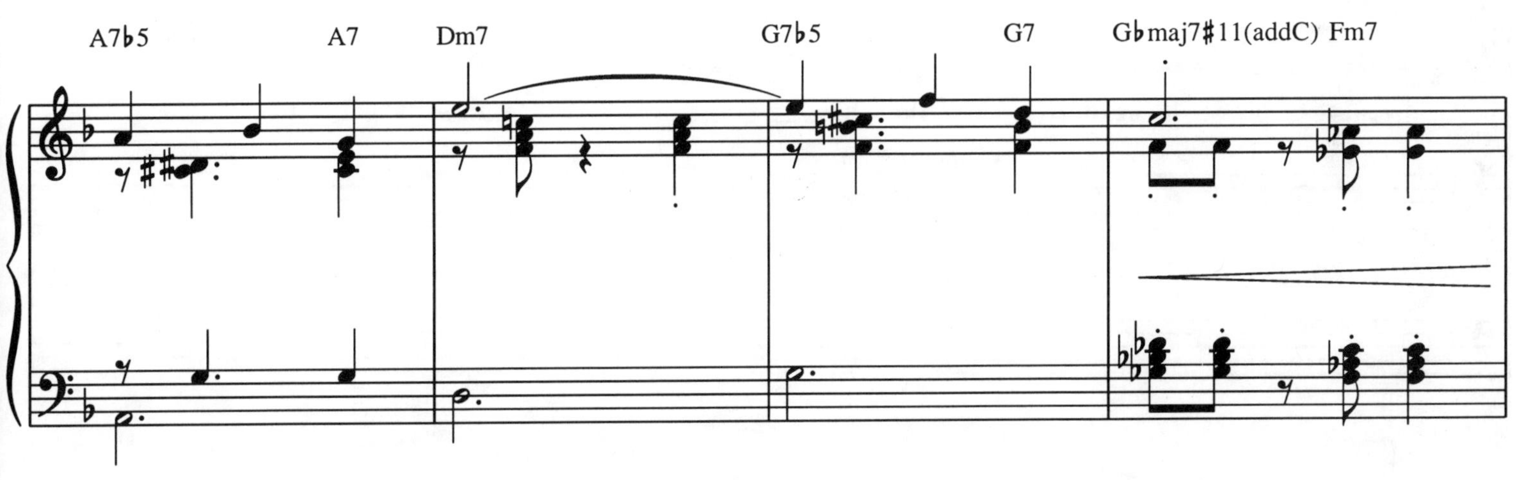
A7♭5
A7
Dm7
G7♭5
G7
G♭maj7♯11(addC)
Fm7

E♭m13
D♭6(addE♭)
C7♯5(♯9)
N.C.
ff
sfz

THE MANY LOVES OF DOBIE GILLIS

Theme Song: Dobie

Lyric by MAX SHULMAN
Music by LIONEL NEWMAN

Gm7
3fr
C7♭9
Fm7
B♭7♭9
size, an - y style, an - y eyes, an - y smile. An - y
E♭
3fr
C7
Fm/B♭
B♭dim7
Fm7/B♭
Adim7
3
Jean, an - y Jane, an - y Joan. Oh,
E♭maj9
E♭6
E♭maj7/G
G♭dim7
Fm7
B♭7
Do - bie wants a girl who's dream-y, Do - bie
Fm7
B♭7♭9
E♭maj9
E♭6
E♭maj9
wants a girl who's cream-y, Do - bie wants a girl to call his own.

Cm
3 fr
F9
F♯dim7
Gm7
3 fr
C7♭9
Is she blond, is she tall, is she
Fm
B♭7♭9
E♭
3 fr
D♭9
C7
dark, is she small, is she an - y kind of dream-boat at all?
No
Fm7
F7
Fm7/B♭
1
E♭6
mat - ter, he's hers and hers a - lone.
Fm7/B♭
B♭9
2
E♭6

McHALE'S NAVY

Theme Song: McHale's Navy March

Music by ALEX STORDAHL

THE MICKEY MOUSE CLUB

Theme Song: Mickey Mouse March

B♭
(Shout) Mick - ey Mouse!
F
(Shout) Don - ald Duck!
Mouse! Mick - ey Mouse! For -
G
G7
C7
(Shout) High! High! High!
ev - er let us hold our ban - ner high!
8va
cresc.
f
F
G7
C7
Come a- long and sing a song and join the jam - bor - ee!
mf
3
F
F7
B♭
B♭m
F
C7
F
M - I - C - K - E - Y M - O - U - S- E!
8va
cresc.
rit.

MISSION: IMPOSSIBLE

Theme Song: Mission: Impossible Theme

By LALO SCHIFRIN

3
f
ff

MISTER ROGERS' NEIGHBORHOOD

Theme Song: Won't You Be My Neighbor?
(It's a Beautiful Day in This Neighborhood)

Words and Music by
FRED ROGERS

A♭m7 D♭ Gm11 C7 F6/9 Cm7 D7
hood with you. So let's make the most of this beau-ti-ful day,
Gm9 B♭m7 F Dm7 Gm7
since we're to-geth-er we might as well say; Would you be mine? Could you be mine?
To Coda
C7 F B♭ Am7 Gm Am7 D7
Won't you be my neigh-bor? Won't you please, won't you please?
Gm7 C7 B♭ F
D.C. al Coda
(with repeat)
Please won't you be my neigh-bor?
CODA
Gm7 C7 B♭ F
Please won't you be my neigh-bor?

THE MONKEES

Theme Song: Theme from "The Monkees"

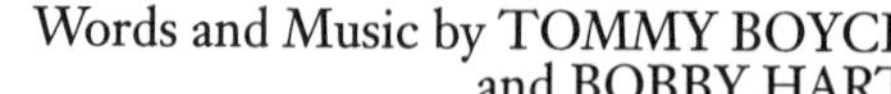
Words and Music by TOMMY BOYCE
and BOBBY HART

Bright rock

Am

Here we come, walkin' down the street.
or any place,

mf

F D

we get the funniest looks from
just look over your shoulder

G7

To Coda

every one we meet.
guess who's standing there.

Hey, hey, we're the Monk-

C
F
G
C
- ees and peo-ple say we mon-key a-round. But
F
G
C
F
G
we're too bus-y sing-ing to put an-y-bod-y down.
1 A
Am
we go where-ev-er we want to,
F
do what we like to do, we don't have time to get

D
G7
rest - less, there's al - ways some-thing new.
2 A
Am
Hey, hey, we're the Monk-
We're just try-in' to be friend -
C
F
G7
C
- ly, come and watch us sing and play.
F
G7
C
We're the young gen - er - a - tion and

F
G7
A
no chord
D.S. al Coda
we got some - thing to say. An - y - time,
CODA
G7
C
F
G
Hey, hey, we're the Monk - ees, you nev - er know where we'll be found,
C
F
G
C
so you'd bet - ter get rea - dy, we
F
G
A
G7
Repeat and Fade
may be com - in' to your town. Hey, hey, we're the Monk -

THE MUNSTERS

Theme Song: The Munsters Theme

By JACK MARSHALL

A7
D7
C7
B7
Em
(Melody)
F
Em
D7
G
D7
G
A7
D7
C7
B7
Em
F
Em
Em
B7
Em
B7
Em

MISTER ED

Theme Song: Mister Ed

Words and Music by JAY LIVINGSTON
and RAY EVANS

G7♭9
G9
G7♯9
G7
you'll en-dorse; He's al - ways on a stead - y course. Talk to Mis - ter
C
F
G♯dim
F
G♯dim
F
G♯dim
Ed! Peo - ple yak - ki - ty yak a streak and waste your time o'
F
C
D♯dim
C
D7
day; But Mis - ter Ed will nev - er speak un - less he has some-thing to
G7
C
G7
say! A horse is a horse, of course, of course, and this one - 'll talk 'til his

G7♭9
G9
G7♯9
G7
G7♭9
G9
voice is hoarse. You nev - er heard of a talk - ing horse?
G7♯9
G7
F♯9
G9
no chord
G7
Well, lis - ten to this, I am
G9
G7♭9
1 C
no chord
G13
Mis - ter Ed!
A
2 C
Dm7
G7
C
Ed!

THE PARTRIDGE FAMILY

Theme Song: Come On Get Happy

Words and Music by WES FARRELL
and DANNY JANSSEN

Eb Bb F Eb Gm
3fr
-py.
We had a dream we'd go
C Eb Bb
trav-elin' to-geth-er we'd spread a lit-tle lov-in' then we'd keep mov-in' on.
Gm C Eb
Some-thin' al-ways hap-pens when-ev-er we're to-geth-er, we get a hap-py feel-in' when we're
Bb Bb F Eb
sing-in' a song. Trav-elin' a-long there's a song that we're sing-in',

Bb
F
Eb
3fr
come on get hap - py.
A
whole lot of lov - in' is what we'll be bring - in',
we'll make you hap - py,
we'll make you hap - py,
we'll make you hap - py.

THE ODD COUPLE

Theme Song: The Odd Couple

Words by SAMMY CAHN
Music by NEAL HEFTI

F7
B7♭5
B♭maj9
B♭6
Em7
A7
As I've in - di - cat - ed they are nev - er
Dm7
G9
B♭maj7
A7♭9
6fr
Dm7
F7
quite sep - a - rat - ed, they are peas in a pod. Don't you think that it's
Em7♭5
A7
Dm7
G7
odd? Their hab - its, I con - fess,
Dm7
G7
Dm7
G7
Dm7
G7
none can guess with the cou - ple. If

Gm7
C7
Gm7
C7
one says no it's yes more or less, with the
Gm7
C7
Gm7
C7
F7
B7♭5
cou - ple. But they're laugh pro -
B♭maj9
B♭6
B♭maj9
A7♭9
vok - ing; yet they real - ly don't
Dm7
F7
B♭6
Gm7
know they're jok - ing. Don't you find when love is

C9sus
1 F
B♭9
A7♭9
6fr
blind it's kind of odd!
No
2 F
B♭m7
F(add9)/A
D7♯9
Gm7
3fr
C7
odd!
Don't you think it's odd?
Gm7
C7
Don't you think it's odd?
Gm7
C7
Don't you think it's odd?
rall.
C6

PERRY MASON

Theme Song: Perry Mason Theme

By FRED STEINER

(senza 8va)
(tr)
(tr)
tr
tr
(con 8va - ad lib.)
2
1.
D. S.
(senza 8va)
2.
sfp
rallent.

THE REAL McCOYS

Theme Song: The Real McCoys

Words and Music by
HARRY RUBY

Gm
3fr
C
F
B♭
for - ni - ay. Ol' Grand - pap - py A - mos and the
gen - tle as a lamb. His grand - son Luke keeps
F
B♭
Gm7
3fr
Gm7/C
1 C7
F
girls and the boys of the fam - i - ly known as The Real Mc - Coys.
beam - ing with joy, since he made Miss Kate Miss - us
2 C7
F
G
C
G
C
Luke Mc - Coy. What a house - keep - er Kate is, she's
Shar - ing each oth - er's sor - rows, en -
G
C
G
D
C
G
do - in' what she en - joys. No gal can beat her when it
joy - in' each oth - er's joys. Like all oth - er fam - 'lies they

C G C G
comes to looks, the same can be said a - bout the
quar - rel and fuss, but it ain't nev - er
Am7 D7 G C
way she cooks for
se - ri - ous, with
Grand - pap - py A - mos and the
G C Am7 Am7/D 1 D7 G
girls and the boys of the fam - i - ly known as The Real Mc - Coys.
2 D7 G G/D D7 G
Real Mc - Coys.

ROUTE 66

Theme Song: Theme from "Route 66"

By NELSON RIDDLE

3
3
1
2

ROCKY & BULLWINKLE

Theme Song: Rocky & Bullwinkle

By FRANK COMSTOCK

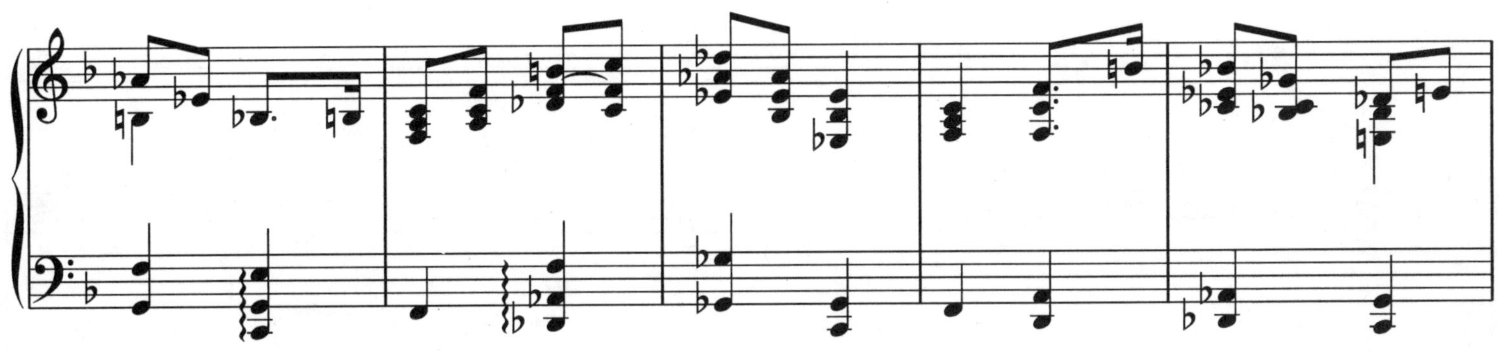

1
2

THE ROY ROGERS SHOW

Theme Song: Happy Trails

Words and Music by
DALE EVANS

E♭
3fr
E♭
3fr
hap - py one for you. Hap - py trails to
Edim7
you un - til we meet a -
B♭7
B♭7sus
B♭7
gain. Hap - py trails to you, keep
B♭7♯5
E♭(add9)
E♭
3fr
smil - in' un - til then. Who

E♭7
A♭maj7
A♭6
3 fr
cares a - bout the clouds when we're to - geth - er? Just
C7
F9
B♭7
sing a song and bring the sun - ny weath - er. Hap - py
E♭
3 fr
B♭m6
6 fr
C7
Fm
B♭7
trails to you till we meet a -
1
E♭
3 fr
B♭7
gain. Hap - py
2
E♭
3 fr
A♭
4 fr
E♭6
gain.

STAR TREK®

Theme Song: Theme from "Star Trek®"

Words by GENE RODDENBERRY
Music by ALEXANDER COURAGE

Db9
Db13#11
4fr
find, in star - clus - tered reach - es,
Eb6
G7#5(#9)
3fr
G7#5
love, strange love a star - wo - man teach - es.
C(add2)
I know his jour - ney ends
Ab13
3fr
C6/9
nev - er; His star trek

F9#11
E9
E9♭5
6fr
will go on for - ev - er.
But
F6
B♭9#11
C6/9
tell him while he wan - ders his star - ry
A7#5(♭9)
Dm7
Dm7/G
sea, Re - mem - ber, re - mem - ber
C6/9
D♭/C
C6/9
me.

77 SUNSET STRIP

Theme Song: 77 Sunset Strip

Words and Music by MACK DAVID
and JERRY LIVINGSTON

G7
A street that wears a fan - cy la - bel,
C
that's glo - ri - fied in song and fa - ble,
G7
the most ex - cit - ing peo - ple pass you by, in -
D7
G7
C
C7
clud - ing a pri - vate eye.
Sev - en - ty sev - en

Gm7
C7
Sun - set Strip, _
sev - en - ty sev - en
Sun - set Strip, _
F7
Cm7
F7
C/E
Dm7
C
sev - en - ty sev - en
Sun - set Strip. _
G7
You'll meet the high - brow and the
hip - ster,
C
the star - let and the pho - ney tip - ster,

G7
D7
G7
you'll find most ev - 'ry kind of gal and guy, in - clud - ing a pri - vate eye.
C
C7
Gm7
C7
Sev - en - ty sev - en Sun - set Strip,
Gm7
C7
F7
sev - en - ty sev - en Sun - set Strip, sev - en - ty sev - en
Cm7
F7
C/E
Dm7
C
Sun - set Strip.

THE TWILIGHT ZONE

Theme Song: The Twilight Zone

By MAURIUS CONSTANT

8va (optional)
Ped.

THE UNTOUCHABLES

Theme Song: Theme from "The Untouchables"

By NELSON RIDDLE

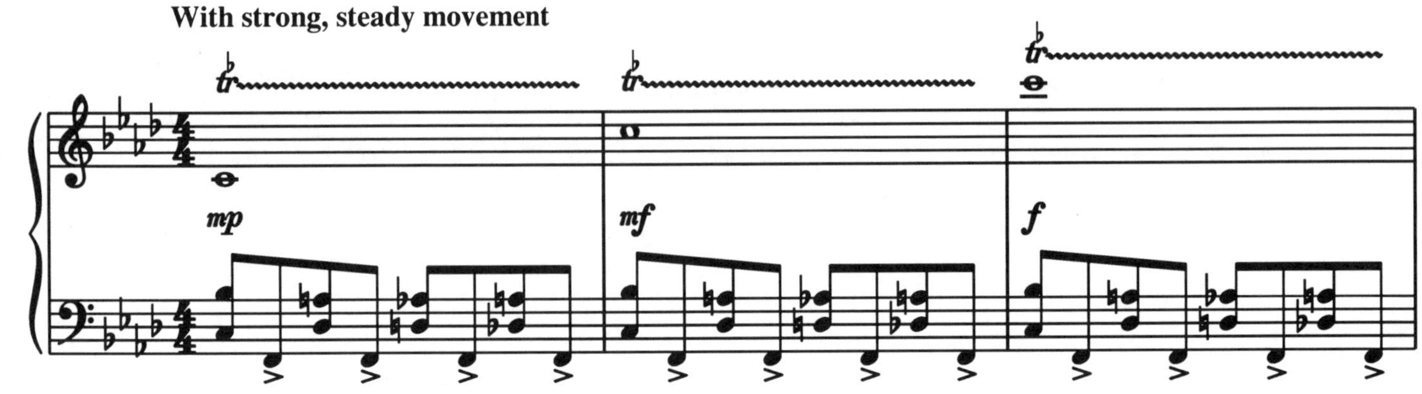

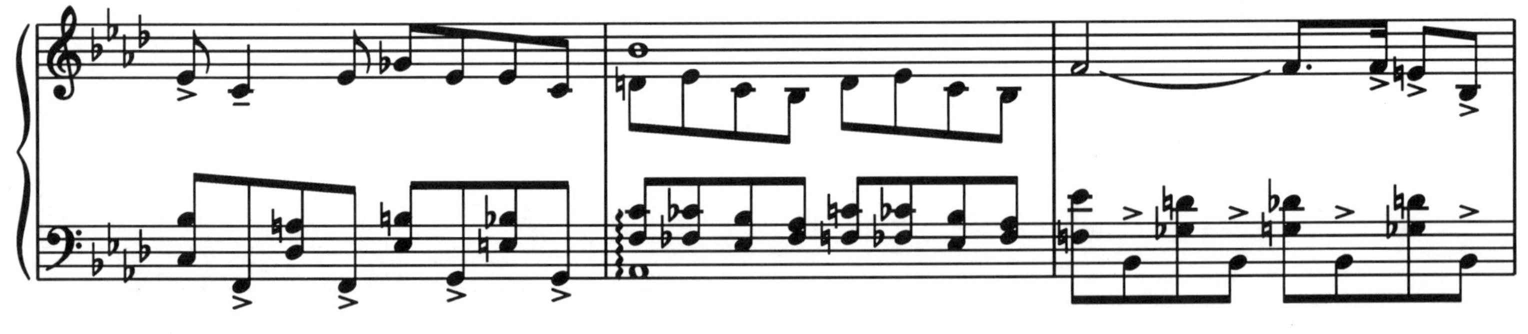

f

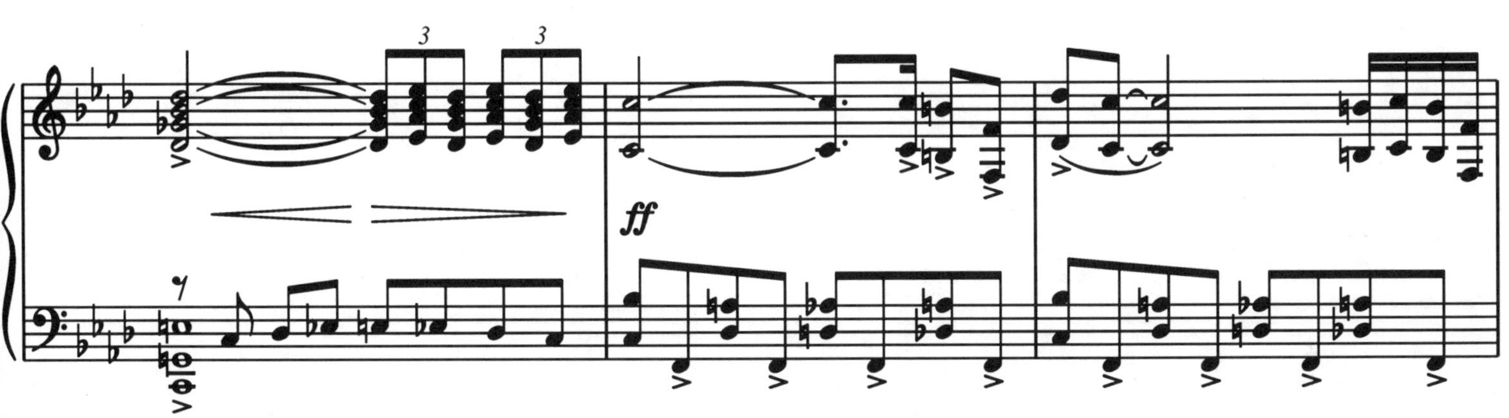
3
3
ff

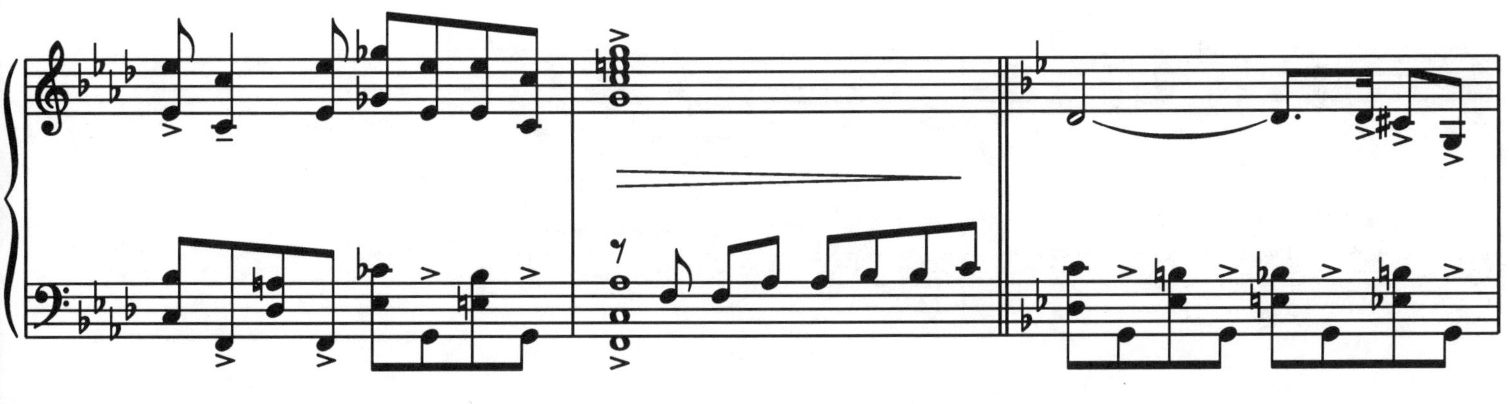

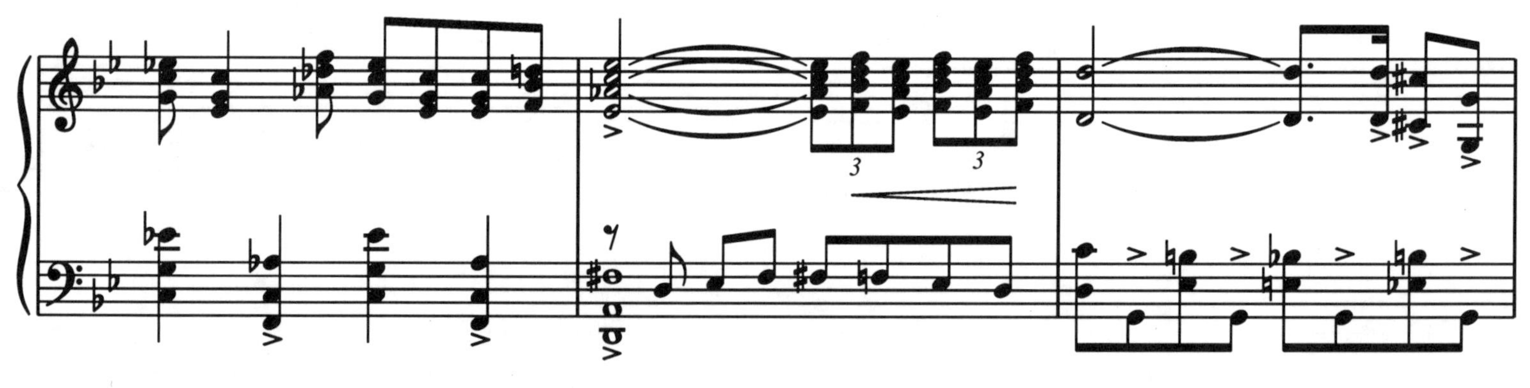

molto rit.

WAGON TRAIN

Theme Song: (Roll Along) Wagon Train

Words by JACK BROOKS
Music by SAMMY FAIN

Fm7
Ab/Bb
roll - in' o - ver moun - tain where there ain't no pass.
won - d'rin' if he's ev - er gon - na shoot you down.
Eb
Gm
Ab
Bb
Sit - tin' on a board, eye - in' the weath - er,
Look - in' for a pal, ain't it a pi - ty,
Eb
Ab
Gm
Ab
Bb9
Eb
To Coda
pray - in' to the Lord, we stay to - geth - er, side by side
look - in' for a gal, need - n't be pret - ty, if she'll ride
Fm7
Ab/Bb
1 Eb6
Fm7
Ab/Bb
on the Wa - gon Train.
Wa - gon

2 E♭6
B♭
Train. Wa - gon ho!
Cm
Gm
Cm7
3 fr
Got - ta keep 'em on the run, time to
Gm
Cm7
F7
B♭
3
go! And fol - low the sun,
B♭7
D.S. al Coda
Roll a -
CODA
Fm7
B♭
B♭7
E♭
on the Wa - gon Train!

THE WONDERFUL WORLD OF DISNEY

Theme Song: When You Wish Upon a Star

Words by NED WASHINGTON
Music by LEIGH HARLINE

Cdim
C
E♭dim
Dm
F
G7
who you are, An - y - thing your heart de - sires will come to
C
G7
C
A7
Dm
Dm7
G7
you. If your heart is in your dream, no re - quest is
Cdim
C
E♭dim
Dm
G7
too ex - treme, When You Wish Up - on A Star as dream - ers
C
Fm6
Em
C
Dm
Gdim
G7
do. Fate is kind, She brings to

Cdim
C
Am
D7
those who love, the sweet ful - fill - ment of their se - cret
Fm6
G7
Abm
G7
C
A7
Dm
Dm7
long - ing. Like a bolt out of the blue,
G7
Cdim
C
Cdim
Dm
Fate steps in and sees you thru, When You Wish Up - on A Star your
1
F
G7
C
G13
2
F
G7
C
dream comes true. dream comes true.

THE WILD WILD WEST

Theme Song: The Wild Wild West Theme

By RICHARD MARKOWITZ

B
C
F
Eb
3fr
F
Bb
A
A7
Dm
Dm/C
Bb
Bb/C
F
Bb/F
F
Bb

A♭
4fr
B♭
D7
Gm
3fr
E♭
3fr
E♭/F
B♭
E♭/B♭
6fr
F
G♭/F
A♭/F
D
C
D
F♯7
Bm
G
G/A
D
Em/D
D

Contemporary Classics

Your favorite songs for piano, voice and guitar.

The Definitive Rock 'n' Roll Collection
A classic collection of the best songs from the early rock 'n' roll years – 1955-1966. 97 songs, including: Barbara Ann • Chantilly Lace • Dream Lover • Duke Of Earl • Earth Angel • Great Balls Of Fire • Louie, Louie • Rock Around The Clock • Ruby Baby • Runaway • (Seven Little Girls) Sitting In The Back Seat • Stay • Surfin' U.S.A. • Wild Thing • Woolly Bully • and more.
00490195 .... $24.95

The Big Book Of Rock
78 of rock's biggest hits, including: Addicted To Love • American Pie • Born To Be Wild • Cold As Ice • Dust In The Wind • Free Bird • Goodbye Yellow Brick Road • Groovin' • Hey Jude • I Love Rock N Roll • Lay Down Sally • Layla • Livin' On A Prayer • Louie Louie • Maggie May • Me And Bobby McGee • Monday, Monday • Owner Of A Lonely Heart • Shout • Walk This Way • We Didn't Start The Fire • You Really Got Me • and more.
00311566.. $19.95

Big Book Of Movie And TV Themes
Over 90 familiar themes, including: Alfred Hitchcock Theme • Beauty And The Beast • Candle On The Water • Theme From *E.T.* • Endless Love • Hawaii Five-O • I Love Lucy • Theme From *Jaws* • Jetsons • Major Dad Theme • The Masterpiece • Mickey Mouse March • The Munsters Theme • Theme From *Murder, She Wrote* • Mystery • Somewhere Out There • Unchained Melody • Won't You Be My Neighbor • and more!
00311582 .... $19.95

The Best Rock Songs Ever
70 of the best rock songs from yesterday and today, including: All Day And All Of The Night • All Shook Up • Ballroom Blitz • Bennie And The Jets • Blue Suede Shoes • Born To Be Wild • Boys Are Back In Town • Every Breath You Take • Faith • Free Bird • Hey Jude • I Still Haven't Found What I'm Looking For • Livin' On A Prayer • Lola • Louie Louie • Maggie May • Money • (She's) Some Kind Of Wonderful • Takin' Care Of Business • Walk This Way • We Didn't Start The Fire • We Got The Beat • Wild Thing • more!
00490424 .... $16.95

The Best Of 90s Rock
30 songs, including: Alive • I'd Do Anything For Love (But I Won't Do That) • Livin' On The Edge • Losing My Religion • Two Princes • Walking On Broken Glass • Wind Of Change • and more.
00311668 .... $14.95

35 Classic Hits
35 contemporary favorites, including: Beauty And The Beast • Dust In The Wind • Just The Way You Are • Moon River • The River Of Dreams • Somewhere Out There • Tears In Heaven • When I Fall In Love • A Whole New World (Aladdin's Theme) • and more.
00311654 .... $12.95

55 Contemporary Standards
55 favorites, including: Alfie • Beauty And The Beast • Can't Help Falling In Love • Candle In The Wind • Have I Told You Lately • How Am I Supposed To Live Without You • Memory • The River Of Dreams • Sea Of Love • Tears In Heaven • Up Where We Belong • When I Fall In Love • and more.
00311670 .... $15.95

The New Grammy® Awards Song Of The Year Songbook
Every song named Grammy Awards' "Song Of The Year" from 1958 to 1988. 28 songs, featuring: Volare • Moon River • The Shadow Of Your Smile • Up, Up and Away • Bridge Over Troubled Water • You've Got A Friend • Killing Me Softly With His Song • The Way We Were • You Light Up My Life • Evergreen • Sailing • Bette Davis Eyes • We Are The World • That's What Friends Are For • Somewhere Out There • Don't Worry, Be Happy.
00359932 .... $12.95

Soft Rock – Revised
39 romantic mellow hits, including: Beauty And The Beast • Don't Know Much • Save The Best For Last • Vision Of Love • Just Once • Dust In The Wind • Just The Way You Are • Your Song.
00311596 .... $14.95

37 Super Hits Of The Superstars
37 big hits by today's most popular artists, including Billy Joel, Amy Grant, Elton John, Rod Stewart, Mariah Carey, Wilson Phillips, Paula Abdul and many more. Songs include: Addicted To Love • Baby Baby • Endless Love • Here And Now • Hold On • Lost In Your Eyes • Love Takes Time • Vision Of Love • We Didn't Start The Fire.
00311539 .... $14.95

FOR MORE INFORMATION, SEE YOUR LOCAL MUSIC DEALER, OR WRITE TO:

HAL•LEONARD™ CORPORATION

7777 W. BLUEMOUND RD. P.O. BOX 13819 MILWAUKEE, WI 53213

Prices, contents & availability subject to change without notice.